$21.50

Chains and Freedom

F

2009

CHAINS AND FREEDOM:

OR,

THE LIFE AND ADVENTURES

OF

PETER WHEELER,

A COLORED MAN YET LIVING.

A SLAVE IN CHAINS,
A SAILOR ON THE DEEP,
AND
A SINNER AT THE CROSS.

THREE VOLUMES IN ONE.

BY

THE AUTHOR OF THE 'MOUNTAIN WILD FLOWER.

———

"Mind not high things; but condescend to men of low estate."
PAUL.

———

NEW-YORK:

PUBLISHED BY E. S. ARNOLD & CO.

1839.

Title Page of *Chains and Freedom*, Library of Congress

Chains and Freedom

Or, The Life and Adventures of Peter Wheeler,
A Colored Man Yet Living.
A Slave in Chains,
A Sailor on the Deep,
and A Sinner at the Cross.

Peter Wheeler

With an introduction
by Graham Russell Gao Hodges

THE UNIVERSITY OF ALABAMA PRESS

Tuscaloosa

Typeface: Caslon

∞

The paper on which this book is printed meets the minimum requirements of
American National Standard for Information Sciences-Permanence of Paper for
Printed Library Materials, ANSI Z39.48-1984.

Library of Congress Cataloging-in-Publication Data

Wheeler, Peter, 1789–1842.
    Chains and freedom : or, the life and adventures of Peter Wheeler, a colored man
yet living. A slave in chains, a sailor on the deep, and a sinner at the cross / Peter
Wheeler ; with an introduction by Graham Russell Gao Hodges.
        p.   cm.
    Amanuensis: Charles Edwards Lester.
    Originally published: New York : E.S. Arnold & Co., 1839.
    Includes bibliographical references.
    ISBN 978-0-8173-5543-2 (pbk. : alk. paper) 1. Wheeler, Peter, 1789–1842.
2. Slaves—New York (State)—Biography. 3. Slaves—New York (State)—Social
life and customs. 4. Slavery—New York (State)—History. 5. New York (State)—
Race relations—History. 6. Slave narratives—New York (State) I. Lester, C. Edwards
(Charles Edwards), 1815–1890. II. Title.
    E444.W56 2009
    306.3'62092—dc22
    [B]

                                                                2009004612

Contents

Acknowledgments

Learning about the stories of Peter Wheeler and Charles Edwards Lester took me to many archives. They include the Columbia County Historical Society, Kinderhook, New York; the Chatham (New York) Public Library; the New York State Library in Albany, New York; the New-York Historical Society; the Rare Book Room at Olin Library, Cornell University; the Rhodes Library at Oxford University, Oxford, United Kingdom; the New Jersey State Library and Archives, Trenton, New Jersey; and the DeWitt Historical Society of Tompkins County, Ithaca, New York. A number of local agencies assisted me, including the Seymour Public Library, Auburn, New York; the Cayuga County Historian's Office; the Cayuga County Clerk's Office; the Tompkins County Clerk's Office; and the DeWitt Historical Society of Tompkins County. Ann Ackerson and her staff at the interlibrary loan service at Colgate University were very helpful, as always. Research for this book was supported by the Discretionary Grant Funds of the Faculty Research Council.

I owe much gratitude to Carol Kammen of Cornell University for suggesting this project and adding encouragement over time. Shane White of the University of Sydney provided me with useful information about Peter Wheeler's life in New York City. Louise Bement, town historian of Lansing, New York, and president of the Lansing Historical Society, was very helpful in finding materials about Gideon Morehouse.

I am deeply grateful to John Brooks of the Department of History at The Ohio State University for sharing with me his valuable research on Columbia County, New York, and for a sharp reading of the introduction. Thanks are also due to the fine staff at The University of Alabama Press.

My wife, Gao Yunxiang, deserves many thanks. This book is dedicated to the memory of Trudy King, the late administrative assistant in the Writing Program at Colgate University. Trudy was immensely valuable in retyping the entire manuscript several times and patiently dealing with corrections. Trudy helped me on a number of publications and always did so with enthusiasm and joy. Her untimely death cut short a life of service and strength.

Chains and Freedom

Introduction

Graham Russell Gao Hodges

On May 5, 1838, Charles Edwards Lester preached his last sermon to his congregation at St. Peter's Presbyterian Church in Spencertown, Columbia County, New York. Overall, Lester claimed, he had been happy in his pastorate and valued the many friends he had gained there. Indeed, there had been a major revival in the area during his tenure. Yet he admitted there had been some unpopular sermons, especially those, he contended, that advocated "the cause of God's suffering and oppressed poor, who are clothed with a dark skin." Lester further pointed out that as a godly cleric, he could not "follow the instructions of men, out of the church, who make no pretensions to religion, respecting the gospel that I preach," an apparent allusion to local animosities toward abolitionism. Lester's church and denomination were undergoing severe strains over the issue of slavery. Conservative Presbyterians did not accept the views of abolitionists like Lester who believed that slaveholding was inherently sinful and unchristian. Equally divisive was the fact that many Presbyterians supported the American Colonization Society's efforts to convince free blacks to choose exile in Africa. In his sermons and writings Lester made plain that he favored the inclusion of blacks in the church as full members. Anything less would deepen the sins of whites and blacks. Lester's words failed to persuade white members of the congregation. Any of the few blacks permitted to attend the church were seated far from the pulpit in "negro pews." When St. Peter's was built in 1808, the trustees assigned "the northwest corner pew in the gallery . . . to the blacks."[1]

In the gallery on the day of Lester's farewell was a forty-nine-year-old African American farmhand named Peter Wheeler. Though their worldly circumstances differed sharply, the youthful cleric and the laborer, who was twice Lester's age, had collaborated on the black man's autobiography, which was published in New York the next year. It was among the first of Lester's many books in a long career, which lasted until his death in 1885. In the case of Peter Wheeler, Lester's book magnified an obscure life into a telling, significant tale of wrongful enslavement, struggle, flight into freedom, and a revealing account of Wheeler's days as a saltwater sailor, servant in New York City, and farmhand. Peter Wheeler's story is packed with wonderful detail about rural black life in the North. It evokes vivid experiences and language while unconsciously revealing the racism of his liberal editor. Within its pages, Wheeler talks of variable interactions with whites, his unlawful enslavement and his day-to-day resistance to servitude, his flight, and his gradual conversion into Christianity, including comments on life and death, damnation, and God's power. The book is unique in its evocation of rural black life in New Jersey and upstate New York.

Sadly, Peter Wheeler's autobiography fell quickly into disuse. Initial advertisements were local. The *Pittsfield (Mass.) Sun* carried notices of the book's publication in the second half of 1839 and into 1840. The Anti-Slavery Bookshop in Boston sold copies in the early 1840s. The book was excerpted in an antislavery anthology in the 1850s but then dropped into oblivion and has never been reprinted in its entirety until now. A reevaluation is overdue. Along with the virtues already mentioned, Peter Wheeler's narrative evokes an enslaved life at the onset of gradual emancipation in New York and New Jersey and documents the powerful tensions between master and slave on the cusp of freedom. It is a valuable source of social history about the lives of free African Americans, their work on farms, in oceanic sailing, and in middle-class parlors of early nineteenth-century New York. Also, it provides a virtually unique vision of the relations between a poor man and the Presbyterian Church. This introduction offers a summary of critical studies of the narrative, provides brief biographical sketches of Wheeler and Lester, discusses useful components of the narrative to modern students, and comments on some of its most controversial elements.

Peter Wheeler and the Critics

Critical appraisal in the century and a half since the initial publication of *Chains and Freedom; Or, The Life and Adventures of Peter Wheeler* has been unkind. Dismissed by Vernon Loggins in an early study in 1931 as "obviously deceptive," and subsequently ignored by succeeding scholars of slave narratives, the book has languished unread.[2] There are additional reasons beyond Loggins's conclusion as to why Peter Wheeler's tale has never been reprinted. Primary was the intrusive presence of his amanuensis, Charles Edwards Lester. Though most slave narratives had some editorial influence, Peter Wheeler's is singular in that Lester is a constant presence in the book. At the close of the first section, for example, Lester adds a number of pages of his own commentary on the debate between abolitionists and adherents of the American Colonization Society. Despite Lester's abolitionism, the book's conclusion may also offer a second reason why the book has remained obscure: Peter Wheeler's autobiography, though antislavery in tone and commentary, recalls more the eighteenth-century tradition of salvation narratives than the politicized antislavery memoirs of the antebellum decades. With the rise of immediatism among antislavery advocates in the 1830s, slave narratives, which came to no other conclusion than an embrace of Christianity, lost credence and influence. As William L. Andrews has pointed out, narrators of the 1840s and beyond prided themselves on hard-won literacy, felt a moral justification based on their activism, and were often ministers, who elevated themselves with the histories of common farmhands like Wheeler. Finally, until very recently, little attention has been given to northern slave narratives because of the paucity of scholarship about servitude above the Mason-Dixon Line and the complacent belief that bondage there was far milder than the crushing subjugation in the South. Closer examination of Wheeler's detailed, evocative narrative offers modern readers full refutation of these beliefs and adds his life journey to the significant accounts by Sojourner Truth, Sylvia Du Bois, John Jea, George White, and other northern blacks.[3]

Peter Wheeler's Life

One of the harshest criticisms of this book is that Lester fabricated it. Fraudulent fugitives preyed upon the abolitionist community in the 1830s and deceived audiences for ill-gotten donations. Fictional slave narratives also appeared in the antebellum period. Proslavery advocates seized upon such books to bolster claims that antislavery attacks were exaggerations or lies. For many generations, historians doubted the veracity or the objective value of narratives as evidence.[4]

Since then, social historians have substantiated much of the personal data in slave narratives. In this instance, tracing Peter Wheeler's life in slavery required merely checking local documents. Peter Wheeler was born enslaved on the farm of Job Mathis in Tuckertown near Egg Harbor, Burlington County, New Jersey, in 1789. Mathis was a prominent area farmer and shipbuilder, who may also have dabbled in the slave trade during the colonial era. Peter probably worked on the Mathis farm on the Bass River in Tuckertown.[5] The Mathis family also owned Peter's sister, Hagar, whom they did not manumit until 1827.[6]

Peter lived his earliest years in Tuckertown. In his wanderings around the area, he encountered wild boars, was attacked by an owl, and caught the devil on a fishing line. His life was not all misery. He enjoyed holidays and tells a humorous anecdote about testimony in Quaker meetings. Wheeler learned to read and write at a local school. Though New Jersey masters were required by law to provide an education to young blacks before freeing them, Peter's time at school was exceptional.

Though he was promised freedom by Job Mathis's will after the decease of Mathis's wife, Leah, which occurred in 1804, Peter remained enslaved by a conspiracy of silence among the estate's executors. The young slave was illegally sold to a man named Gideon Morehouse. Despite the desperate efforts of his sister, Hagar, who tried to purchase him from Morehouse, Peter's new owner forced the youthful black man to travel with him to Cayuga County on the frontier of upstate New York. The kidnapping and forcible sale of young blacks to remote regions was unfortunately common in New Jersey, where the legislature had just passed a bill enabling gradual emancipation that year. Under the terms of the act, Peter Wheeler, born before the effective date of July 4, 1804, was a slave for life, though his master's will nullified that status. Still, because the family did not register his manumission, the executors could freely sell him out of the state without legal recrimination.[7]

Morehouse was one of many farmers who, crowded at home, moved to the Genesee frontier in upstate New York to develop its fertile land. Morehouse chose the location because his brother, Pierson Morehouse, had already settled there. Exactly when Morehouse and Peter Wheeler arrived in Cayuga County is unclear; local sources indicate 1800 as the date, but dating their arrival in that year conflicts with the death of Peter's mistress in New Jersey four years later. At any rate, Morehouse soon owned several plots in Genoa and Trumansberg; he appears on the 1810 census for Genoa. Morehouse's first wife, Phoebe, died in 1812; he remarried to Lecta Conger Morehouse, the widow of his brother Pierson, the following year. Lecta is mentioned in the narrative for helping Peter save money, which

Peter Wheeler, Library of Congress

was then confiscated by his master. The couple had seven children and became an important stem family in the community. The main portion of
Morehouse's property was located along the Salmon River. In 1817, by previous agreement, Genoa split into several parts, and Morehouse's land became part of what would become the village of Ludlowville in Lansing
Township, Tompkins County. Morehouse grew to be a fairly well known
citizen and trustee of the First Presbyterian Church of Ludlowville.[8]

Although he taught Peter carpentry and farm skills, Morehouse inter-
spersed these lessons with physical brutality. Wheeler and Lester surely
intended to show that the remnants of northern slavery could be just as
cruel as the more notorious southern system, for their account of Peter's
time with Morehouse is studded with descriptions of whippings and other
beatings. From the first days, Morehouse proved to be a thuggish master,
intent on beating Peter into submission. To get Peter to cut wood to build
a new house, Morehouse whipped the bondsman. He also took Peter's re-

wards for killing a poisonous snake and for saving a neighbor's daughter from drowning. Morehouse could act freely because the property rights of masters were respected on the frontier. There were about sixteen slaves in Ludlowville, including Peter, around 1806.[9]

The presence of slavery did not please all residents. Sympathetic whites encouraged Peter Wheeler to show Morehouse "your backsides," by running away. A landlord, Mr. Cooper, told Peter that it was illegal to bring slaves from another state to New York, a law tested in 1800. Several other whites counseled Peter on his potential freedom. While Peter helped Morehouse construct his home, white day laborers advised him to "show Morehouse the bottoms of your feet." The Tooker family (Tucker in the narrative), whose daughter Peter saved from drowning, were members of the abolitionist-minded Methodist Church. They openly advised Peter to flee. A local squire told Peter he was free. Peter and Squire Whittlesey agreed he should not run away until the young man knew more about the world. Their testimony indicates the shift in New York's western counties against enslavement. Widespread along the Hudson River and in the cities of Albany and New York, slavery was gradually abolished after 1799 in New York State. Like New Jersey, though, the Empire State required enslaved blacks born before the effective date of gradual emancipation to serve their masters for the rest of their lives. As its economy moved toward free wage labor, New York's frontier residents split their opinions about slavery, usually over religious grounds. For example, in Ludlowville, Methodists opposed human bondage while Presbyterians tolerated it. Later, the entire region became avowedly antislavery.[10]

Peter's determination to mature before taking leave of Morehouse brought him a number of skills and endurance for hard work. The enslaved black's labors were arduous. He tells of helping Morehouse construct his home by hewing timber and lifting each log into place. Peter and his master fished and hunted together. Morehouse also rented Peter to nearby whites, a violation of the 1800 decision that a few years later brought freedom to Austin Steward, another black narrator, who lived only about forty miles from Peter Wheeler. Morehouse's brutality disgusted his white neighbors, who actively urged Peter to flee. Morehouse imprisoned Peter, starved him, and took his animal skins without payment (a violation of customary master/slave relations). Relations turned worse after Peter found religion at a camp meeting. Although Morehouse kept whipping him, Peter began to contemplate his position. During the winter, when the sadistic Morehouse tried to strike him with a pitchfork,

Peter responded by hitting his master across the back with a stake. More-house then threatened Peter with a gun, upon which the young bondsman knocked him aside and demanded a pass to find a new master.

Fortunately for Peter, another white prosecuted Morehouse for cruelty. The master was found guilty and fined five hundred dollars. With his judgments about Morehouse affirmed in a court of law, Peter decided to leave his master. He had planned his escape for several years, but used the eclipse of 1806 as a sign that the time was right for freedom.[11] Peter Wheeler's flight was actually fairly easy. Helpful whites enabled his journey by wagon, foot, canal boat, and riverboat across upstate New York, through Utica, to Albany, and down to New York City. There were a few close calls, but friendly New Yorkers warned Peter of any incipient dangers. In Albany he got a job as a cook on a riverboat at ten dollars per month, only to learn that Gideon Morehouse was searching for him. The captain, a John Truesdell, even showed him a fugitive slave advertisement.

Truesdell's kindness was opportune because shortly after Peter's arrival in New York City, he was arrested for stealing about $125 in notes and fifty pieces of silver from a Jonathan Blackner of Dorset, Vermont. Blackner claimed that Peter had stolen the money from him while both were on a sloop docked off the First Ward in the city. Peter was indicted, but no record of his conviction exists. Had he been found guilty, he probably would have had to serve at least three months in the new state prison in Greenwich Village.[12]

Truesdell then employed Peter on a deep-sea voyage, leaving New York for St. Bartholomew on October 22, 1806. From there Peter traveled to Puerto Rico. He spent the winter of 1806–1807 in New York, working as a servant in a wealthy man's home. Neither job was uncommon for a young black man. Jeffrey Bolster estimates that as many as 18 percent of sailors shipping from New York in the first decades of the nineteenth century were black, and historians generally agree that blacks dominated the domestic trade in the city until 1825.[13]

In succeeding seasons, Peter sailed as part of Truesdell's crew to England, Gibraltar, and Amsterdam. On one voyage they encountered a slave ship, where Peter sadly viewed the chained bondspeople. That experience impressed upon his mind the shared misery of enslaved Africans. Back home, his life was improving. Working for several ship captains, he had saved several hundred dollars in New York City banks, though that cash was soon lost in a bad investment. Over the next few years he alternated between domestic work in the city and seafaring, including travels into the

Mediterranean and back to England. By 1812 he was back in New York and by his own account went through a period of depravity and drunkenness.

Work enabled Peter to stay afloat financially. He toiled as a domestic for a wealthy Quaker woman in New York and for a family in Philadelphia. There he fell in love with and was engaged to a young free black woman named Solena, only to have her die in his arms. His sorrow pushed Peter on the road again, to New York and New Haven. Another female friend of his, Susan Macy, told him of her kidnapping from the streets of New York. He was in Hartford, Connecticut, in 1815 during the Federalist convention, and then followed a servant's route through New England, staying a year in Middletown, Connecticut; a few months in West Springfield, Massachusetts; and then back to New York City and western Massachusetts.

Around 1825 Peter Wheeler arrived in Spencertown, a farm hamlet attached to the village of Austerlitz in Columbia County, New York, near the eastern border with Massachusetts. Spencertown was fairly independent and possessed a cider mill, cooperage and carpentry shops, general store, shoe shops, and wharves for easy transit of goods to Hudson and New York. At the center of the town were the Presbyterian church, originally formed as a Methodist parish in the 1770s, and the Spencertown Academy, a noted preparatory school. Peter Wheeler is listed in the 1830 census for Austerlitz and probably lived near the highway running from Hartford, Connecticut, to Albany. African Americans constituted only 2 percent of Austerlitz's population and faced very limited economic destinies. Most blacks in the town were young laborers (Wheeler was one of only three blacks over the age of thirty-six), living as dependents on farms. In the 1830 census, 82 percent of the African Americans living in Columbia County were agricultural laborers.

As with virtually all other blacks males in the county, Peter Wheeler never owned property in Spencertown. Doubtless he worked primarily as a dependent laborer, or "cottager," a pattern that was standard for Hudson Valley communities, where few people of color had freeholds in the first decades after the Gradual Emancipation Act of 1799. The town did have some black notables, including a cooper named Joe Wing. Several of the black homes near the highway were known stops on the Underground Railroad.[14]

Despite his dependent status, Peter Wheeler settled in Spencertown. Evidence of his acceptance in the town comes from the "Certificate of the Citizens of Spencertown," in which the townspeople affirmed their knowledge of Peter and their belief in the veracity of his statements. A necessary accoutrement of black narratives, such affidavits legitimized them. The exposé of the narrative of James Williams (published in 1838), which proslavery Alabama whites had demonstrated was fraudulent, had embarrassed the abolition movement. Although little evidence of deceptive writing has surfaced, racist and proslavery whites used the Williams episode to denigrate the slave narrative as a genre, a suspicion that has plagued historical researchers ever since. Lester and Wheeler were surely aware of contemporary skepticism, so the list of Peter's supporters is impressive. Among the signers are the two local justices of the peace, the Presbyterian church deacon, a doctor, and members of the leading families of Spencertown, men whose roots in the community went back to the hamlet's founding in the eighteenth century. At the bottom of the list is a statement that many of them had known Wheeler for "more than thirteen years," or at least since his arrival in 1825. The narrative indicates that he had known Justice Pratt even before then. It is not difficult to imagine that all of these people had heard Wheeler's tales during breaks from the plow or during community gatherings.[15]

Certainly one religious practice bonded Wheeler to his friends at St. Peter's. Charles Davenport's reminiscences of Spencertown include vivid recreations of services and choir singing. Services were morning and afternoon, with an intermission for Sunday school and lunch. According to Davenport, the choir was a chief attraction at St. Peter's. During services the choir sat behind the minister, separated from him by a green curtain fastened to an iron rod by brass rings. As the hymn was announced, the curtain was drawn, hiding the choir. The choir leader selected suitable tunes from a large selection of anthems, quartets, and choruses. The leader would then find the appropriate key by using a tuning fork or a pitch horn, and would give the first note of his or her part. Then the choir arose with head and shoulders above the green curtain. They were accompanied by musicians using a Melophone (an instrument like a melodeon), a tall bass viol, and a violin and flute. The choir was talented enough to garner invitations to sing throughout the area. Though the minister in an evangelical church was important, St. Peter's experienced frequent turnover of pastors. Moreover, some of Lester's messages about the iniquity of slavery were not well received, and he left the church after only two years. In such a church, a dynamic choir, replete with its own ritual and powerful musical instruments, occupied center stage during services and probably eclipsed the minister.[16]

However welcoming was the Presbyterian church to blacks, fellowship usually ended at the parish door. Black worshippers were relegated to "negro pews," which were located in galleries or far from the front of the church. The negro pew was the worst of insults to black Christians. In the cities, few whites would ever publicly sit with a black congregant. Arthur Tappan caused a furor by bringing the black Presbyterian minister Samuel E. Cornish into the whites-only Laight Street Presbyterian Church in New York City. This act of benevolence was considered a partial cause of the race riots of 1834. Sadly, Peter's references to the "nigger pew" indicate that his fate mirrored his urban counterparts. In the narrative he plaintively asks Lester how Christians could bar a fellow adherent from common worship. His narrative suggests, moreover, that he had a fine singing voice and knowledge of many tunes. Lester asks him to sing sailors' chants and quotes his songs in full. The lines between sacred and secular tunes often blurred in evangelical denominations, and it is hard to believe that a man with Wheeler's vocal talents would not be a match for those of the choir, though it is doubtful that he sang in the church's musical features.[17]

Despite these frustrations, Wheeler worked for Erastus Pratt for a number of years, an employment that secured him an important local ally. By 1830 Wheeler was a family man with a wife named Sylvia. Their only child died as an infant. Until Lester came along to record his story, Wheeler's personal saga was limited by his surroundings. Once encouraged by his editor, Wheeler poured out his tales. His memoirs were published about three years before his death on March 2, 1842. Halfway across New York State, Gideon Morehouse died a year later, on March 5, 1843.[18]

Charles Edwards Lester

As noted, Wheeler's amanuensis, Charles Edwards Lester, was at the beginning of a distinguished career as a historian when he met the former slave. Lester, descended from Jonathan Edwards on the maternal side, was born in 1815 in Griswold, Connecticut. He was first admitted to the bar in New York State, but then spent two years at Auburn Theological Seminary and began to preach. Lester met Wheeler during the former's brief employment as pastor of St. Peter's Presbyterian Church in Spencertown. Undoubtedly, he saw the rural post as a good place to begin his career. Columbia County was the home of Martin Van Buren, then-president of the United States, and was quite prosperous. Working at St. Peter's as minister from 1836 to 1838, Lester wrote his earliest publications. In addition to

Charles Edwards Lester, by Matthew Brady, Library of Congress

his editorial work on Wheeler's autobiography, the young cleric penned a four-hundred-page memoir of Mrs. Mary Ann Bise, a local wife and saintly parishioner who had died at twenty-three.[19]

Forced to abandon the ministry because he was experiencing pulmonary hemorrhages, Lester first moved to Utica, New York, and may have encountered the famed abolitionist Alvan Stewart. Lester next attended the World Anti-Slavery Convention in London in 1840. His activities at the conference included reading a paper on the conditions of free blacks in Canada and supporting a measure describing how the Hudson Bay Company of Canada permitted enslavement of Native Americans, an abuse that Lester argued should be brought to the attention of the English government. While in London he also wrote an impassioned broadside proclaiming the virtues of the fugitive slave communities coalescing in Upper Canada (Ontario) as well as the bravery of Hiram Wilson, who left Lane Seminary in Ohio after that school refused to admit blacks.[20]

During his time in England, Lester published a controversial history titled *The Glory and Shame of England* (1841), in which he derided British institutions and government but praised the United States. A Scottish abolitionist, Peter Brown, responded in his own book, *The Fame and Glory of England Vindicated,* by denouncing American slavery and lauding English institutions, an argument that played far better with American antislavery activists than Lester's timid arguments. Brown was much more in touch with American antislavery beliefs by contending that American slavery was a fatal weakness to the nation's advance toward liberty, the ultimate goal of any state. He further pointed out that Lester was strangely passive about slavery and was deferential in a letter to John C. Calhoun, the apostle of proslavery. In this communication Lester urged Calhoun to consider the idea that slavery's extinction might benefit slaveholders and that it avoided a well-established belief that slavery violated God's instructions. Lester also criticized British merchants for buying slave-grown cotton and the English government for permitting its importation. Later, Lester disparaged British emancipation, contending that compensation of twenty million pounds had severely burdened English taxpayers. Brown's rebuttal of Lester gained him a rising reputation while Lester moved into other literary venues.[21]

Nonetheless, the African American press reacted favorably to Lester's work, although no review of Wheeler's story can be found. Soon, however, Lester gained some credence with black abolitionists. Though he angered English activists, *The Glory and Shame of England* received strong words of praise in the *Colored American.* The reviewer proclaimed: "We know not when we have perused a work with more profound interest." Noting that many American writers had portrayed England, Lester, the notice said, wrote from the "movings of humanity" about Britain's "starving millions who could only be compared with "our own American slavery." This review was but one of many to praise Lester's work, and *The Glory and Shame* made his reputation.[22]

Lester's public career took another upswing in 1843 when he was appointed U.S. consul to Genoa, Italy, where he served six years, an experience he related in his memoirs (*My Consulship,* 2 vols., 1853). During his stay in Genoa he also wrote a history of Christopher Columbus titled *The Artist, Merchant, and Seaman* (1845). After his return to America, he settled in New York City and commenced a literary life. In rapid succession, he authored hefty studies of *Americus Vespucci* (1846), the *Napoleon Dynasty* (1852), and *Glances at the Metropolis* (1854). He translated several Italian works into English, including Machiavelli's *Florentine History* (1846). Later he wrote a biography of Charles Sumner (1874), a study of the Civil War (1878), *The Mexican Republic* (1878), and a two-volume *History of the United States* (1883). He died in 1885 after having published twenty-seven books and translated a number of French and Italian works.[23]

It was not unusual for an ambitious professional writer like Lester to tackle the job of transcribing a slave narrative. Nor was his method unique. Lester, like many other amanuenses, lived in the same locale as his subject. A member of his church, Wheeler was doubtless pleased and secure about telling his life story to the young minister. Wheeler regularly visited Lester, who took down his account verbatim. Later, Lester added his own commentary, linking Wheeler's tale with larger philosophical and theological issues and using the laborer's experiences to illustrate the iniquity of slave masters and traders. Cognizant of the controversial nature of the book, as its time of publication loomed, Lester persuaded a number of prominent local citizens to add testimonials to the effort's veracity.[24]

By 1852 Lester had alienated the black press. The reactions to his new work perhaps foreshadowed the neglect Peter Wheeler's story would receive in the future. The furious decade of the 1850s started out amicably between Lester and the abolitionist movement. He collaborated with Matthew Brady, the famous daguerrotypist and photographer, to produce *The Gallery of Illustrious Americans* (1850), which the *National Era* praised, though the reviewer concentrated on the portraits. Lester's lush volume appealed not so much to his erstwhile colleagues in the abolitionist movement, but to new friends among New York's mercantile elite. As Mary Panzer notes, Lester attracted an audience made up principally of wealthy manufacturers and merchants. He repaid them by promoting "pianos, carpets, wallpaper, mirrors, picture frames, silverware, prints, dry-good stores, sellers of books and magazines, daguerrotypists, and manufacturers of cast iron, safes, and steam engines."[25]

Within two years the abolitionist press ostracized Lester. He had initiated a new magazine called the *Herald of the Union*, which, in its first issue, offered to mediate the growing crisis over the Compromise of 1850. The *National Era*, which had lauded his previous effort, described the magazine as "in favor of the Union, the Compromise, Slavery, and Constructive Treason." It noted that Lester was a famous man and that "if he had

as much nerve as impudence, would make quite a respectable hangman."
In his paper, Frederick Douglass praised the magazine's format as "exceed-
ingly prepossessing" and "highly finished, clear, white, strong and beautiful, and . . . unsurpassed." Inside, however, "its beauty is like that of a certain venomous reptile, which fascinates but to sting and poison." Never
was there a "more base, cringing, profligate sycophant" than Lester, who
once was "professedly an abolitionist." Now no longer employed by the
government, he was desperate and ready to sell his soul. Douglass doubted
that "even the worst class of Americans can have stomach" for him and his
magazine. After this angry denunciation, Lester's name disappeared from
the abolitionist press as his enthusiasm for ending slavery waned.[26]

Peter Wheeler's Narrative as Historical Document and Literature

Not many slave narratives have literary merit. Frederick Douglass, Harriet
Jacobs, Sojourner Truth, and William Wells Brown are among the few
black narrators whose works appeal as literature to twentieth-century
readers. Charles Lester and Peter Wheeler composed the latter's narrative a year before the historian became known in abolitionist and literary
circles. There are stylistic elements of the narrative, however, that would
become controversial. Its sentimental, ornate style is perhaps grating to
modern ears but was fairly common for the antebellum period. More difficult, however, was the use that Lester and Wheeler make of the pejo-
rative term "nigger." Now one of the most taboo words in the English
language, the term had then only recently emerged from the Dutch ver-
nacular, a tongue Wheeler and Lester heard daily in the Upper Hudson
Valley. The *Oxford English Dictionary* cites its use in 1786, and again in 1811
and 1819. Words become adopted into use quickly, and the 1830s saw a rising current of racism in New York. Still, this is the only narrative in which
the subject and the editor make common use of the term. It is impossible to know whether or not Lester knew of Hosea Easton's condemna-
tion of the word, published in 1837 in his treatise on blacks in the United
States.[27] For Wheeler, its use seems so frequent as to hardly merit men-
tion; for Lester, it signified his anger over slavery. To modern readers, its
occurrence is offensive and difficult to read. On the one hand, it reflects
the crudeness of Wheeler's life, for he rarely had contact with educated
people. In fact, his contacts with whites largely consisted of the vicious
Morehouse and hearty but crude sea captains and farmers. Lester's use of

the epithet indicates a racial ambivalence, which Douglass later discerned in the historian.[28]

Wheeler's narrative is more assured than most of its genre. Beyond the prefatory list of citizens of Spencertown, who may also have underwritten the costs of publication, there is little about Wheeler's narrative that suggests anxiety over authenticity, a factor that is evident in, for example, the narrative of Solomon Northrup. Nor is there a self-effacing quality, which may be found in the narratives of Charles Ball, a book that Wheeler enjoyed, and in William Grimes's story. In fact, Wheeler seems at home with his life.[29] The construction of Wheeler's narrative is rather complex. It is composed of three linked "books," or sections, each with lengthy notes revealing Lester's opinions on slavery, the slave trade, colonization, and racism. Within each section Peter Wheeler relates his stories directly to his amanuensis, Lester, who then transcribed them. Wheeler clearly enjoyed telling his tales, and it was always Lester who tired and ended each session. While Wheeler respectfully addressed Lester as *Domine,* the Dutch term for "minister," there is never a moment in the narrative in which the black man was servile or deferential.

The narrative includes good descriptions of Wheeler's work life on the farm, at sea, and as an urban domestic. It is replete with portrayals of the savage brutality of Morehouse, the slave master. Wheeler and his amanuensis created a classic villain in Morehouse, who kidnapped his chattel, stole his possessions, humiliated him, and in every way denigrated his humanity. There are discussions by Wheeler and Lester about the iniquity of stealing a man as property and invocations of a labor theory of value. Subsequently, however, whites treated Peter Wheeler fairly, helping him on numerous occasions to avoid recapture by Morehouse. Peter's resistance of his enslavement included day-to-day actions and culminated in his directly confronting Morehouse. It is impossible to know if Frederick Douglass read Wheeler's narrative before composing his own classic history in 1845, but the northern bondsman's physical battle with his master anticipates the great abolitionist's own description of his fights with Mr. Edward Covey, the "negro-breaker." Perhaps the greatest difference between the two narratives is that Wheeler saw Morehouse as a singular violator of Christian ethics while Douglass used Mr. Covey to represent all sinners within a Christianity adrift from its original tenets.[30]

It is that collision of Peter Wheeler's beliefs that makes his narrative so interesting. Wheeler's tale followed a road to salvation trod by many black narrators and blazed by other Protestants as far back as John Bunyan. His narrative tells not only of the journeys that potential Christians make en route to their faith but also of the picaresque adventures they encounter and the pathways not taken.[31] It is particularly noteworthy that Wheeler's narrative is by a black adherent of the Presbyterian Church, a denomination that has been studied for its effects on educated blacks. During the 1830s the Presbyterian Church was ambivalent about African Americans. On the one hand, it was the leading supporter of the American Colonization Society, which northern free blacks detested. The Presbyterians split over the issue of slavery, with more conservative congregations supporting conciliatory positions toward the South and slavery, while the northern church promoted the colonization society as the answer to the problem of slavery. Its evangelical methods placed it along with Methodism and Baptism in its outreach to blacks. Some of the most significant black abolitionists, including James W. C. Pennington and Samuel E. Cornish, were Presbyterian ministers.[32]

Wheeler's narrative is the best source for understanding his religious beliefs. His first exposure to Christianity was contradictory. Morehouse was a Quaker, but by Wheeler's estimation, not a true adherent. Morehouse refused to accept the edicts of the Society of Friends to cut all ties to the system of slavery and so left the church to join the Presbyterians. Wheeler also received instruction in his distant African past from his mother, who told him that their great-grandfather was born in Africa and had been stolen from the seaside by traders. These first influences were inconclusive. His African heritage had become distant, though not lost, while the Quakers' primary quest to cleanse the stain of slavery from Christian life had little real meaning for the young slave. Stronger in impact were the camp meetings he attended as a young man in upstate New York at Plane Hill near Auburn, New York. At one event Peter asked the meeting to pray for him because he was trying to grasp the swirling events around him. The worshippers formed a "prayin' circle" led by an aged man of color. Peter was told to go to his knees as the adherents prayed, shouted, sang, and clapped their hands. This Pentecostal event is remarkably similar to the "ring shout" found by Sterling Stuckey to be central to the African American religious experience.[33] What is surprising in Wheeler's narrative is that he rejects the emotional fervor and wants more than anything to escape quickly. He observes: "Prayin' in the woods makes me think of bein' *tied up* there." This statement initially separates Wheeler from many black Christian narrators who gained contact with God not in church, but in a natural surrounding. Throughout most of his narrative, Wheeler views nature as hostile. He was attacked by owls, fought snakes and bears, and, most significantly, was left tied to a tree by the sadistic Morehouse after a whipping. Some of this may be attributed to the sensible concerns a farmworker would have about the dangers of nature, but Wheeler was so damaged by Morehouse's brutality that he initially rejected African spirituality and Christian evangelical love.

There was little during his early life to bring Peter Wheeler to faith. It is remarkable, however, that it was an eclipse that prompted him to flee from Morehouse. Americans of all creeds viewed such signs as spiritual events. Even though the moon was bright on the evening of his flight, Wheeler was troubled by night sounds and fears of poisonous snakes. Beyond the fears Wheeler had of nature, he does include remarkable passages describing how settlers in the Genesee region carved out an existence. He tells of building a cabin, cutting wood, and planting fields. He encounters Native Americans. These descriptions are particularly unusual in northern slave narratives, which are generally focused on urban life or the sea. While Wheeler spends ample time telling about his years on the ocean, the bulk of the narrative is about rural life. Some of Wheeler's tales are confirmed by the memories of other townspeople. His tale of building the Morehouse home is close to other accounts. Similarly, Peter's recollections of General Training Day match those of local historians. The Tooker family reminiscences include the story of the infant charmed by the rattlesnake as well as the general anxieties caused by the snakes. Last, Peter's fondness for singing is matched by the recollections of other local African Americans.[34]

After relating his freedom journey, Peter Wheeler felt more comfortable interspersing his narrative with side comments about religion and slavery. An important discussion concerns the negro pew. After some insightful commentary about racist attitudes among the people to whom he serves food, Wheeler sadly describes the segregation of communion at St. Peter's: "All communicants was axed to come and partake together, and I come down from the gallery, and as I come into the door, to go and set down among 'em; one of the elders stretched out his arm, with an air of disdain, and beckoned me away to a corner pew."

Similar exclusion existed, Wheeler realized, in the cemetery. He struggled mightily with the depressing power of these insults to his faith. Gradually, he came to "submit to my fate; and I believed God could see me, and hear my cry, and accept my love, as well there as though I sot in the midst on 'em." Rather than reject religion as he had as a young man,

Wheeler blamed northern racism for the "reason why the people of our colour don't rise any faster."

Peter Wheeler's comments indicate that despite his economic status and remote existence, he did hold political views about slavery and the slave trade. He was aware of other narratives, knew about the sufferings of English abolitionist George Thompson, commented on the negro pew, and discussed vividly his witness of the terrors of a slave ship. Wheeler was deeply troubled by the sight of Africans writhing in the hold of a slave ship at sea. This experience strengthened his aversions to slavery, a feeling that previously had been only individual. Seafaring did little for his religious development; indeed, Peter Wheeler describes himself as depraved in these years.

Even after he left the sea and worked as a domestic in New York City, Wheeler regarded himself as a sinner. Following the sudden death of his fiancée, Solena, which caused grief for many years, Peter wandered through the northeast, working at many jobs for many employers as a town-to-town migrant. Eventually he found himself in Spencertown, where his faith became visible. During the revival of 1827–1828, Peter attended prayer meetings at both the Pratt and Mayhew homes. The revivals so affected him that he cried in public. His subsequent conversion was remarkable. Unable to speak publicly because of fear that his blackness would condemn him in the eyes of other parishioners, Wheeler walked home alone. He came to a large flat rock, and there "'twas the *first time I ever raly prayed.*" He spoke directly to God and asked his help to "do my duty, and submit to let you dispose on me jist as you please, for time and eternity." He got up from the rock and the "world did look beautiful round me." Wheeler then went home, awakened his wife and mother-in-law, and read the fourteenth chapter of John to them. Wheeler had found happiness in his own family rather than at the church. His fusion of African theology (the rock), acceptance of nature, and embrace of family helped Peter Wheeler accept his two-ness in the world: as a black man and as a Christian American. His history deepens understanding of W. E. B. Du Bois's concept of the double veil by demonstrating how a single black man, living in a somewhat hostile, rural society, retained his Africanity within a white Protestant denomination.[35]

Chains and Freedom

Or, The Life and Adventures
of
Peter Wheeler,
A Colored Man Yet Living.

A Slave in Chains,
A Sailor on the Deep,
and
A Sinner at the Cross.

Three Volumes in One.
By
The Author of the Mountain Wild Flower

~

"Mind not high things; but condescend to men of low estate."

PAUL.

Preface

The following Narrative was taken entirely from the lips of Peter Wheeler. I have in all instances given his own language, and faithfully recorded his story as he told it, *without any change whatever.* There are many astonishing facts related in this book, and before the reader finishes it, he will at least feel that "Truth is stranger than fiction."

But the truth of every thing here stated can be relied on. The subject of this story is well known to the author, who for a long time brake unto him "the bread of life," as a brother in Christ, and beloved for the Redeemer's sake. There are, likewise, hundreds of living witnesses, who have for many years been acquainted with the man, and aware of the incidents here recorded, who cherish perfect confidence in his veracity.

He has many times, for many years, related the same facts, to many persons, in the same language *verbatim;* and individuals to whom the author has read some of the following incidents, have recognized the story and language, as they heard them from the hero's lips long before the author ever heard his name. There are also persons yet living, whom I have seen and known, who witnessed many of Peter's most awful sufferings.

Of course, the book lays no claim to the merit of *literature,* and will not be reviewed as such; but it does claim the merit of *strict verity,* which is no mean characteristic in a book, in these days.

The subject, and the author, have but one object in view in bringing the book before the public: a mutual desire to contribute as far as they can, to the freedom of enchained millions for whom Christ died. And if any heart may be made to feel one emotion of benevolence, and lift up a more earnest cry to God for the suffering slave; if one generous impulse may be awakened in a slaveholder's bosom towards his fellow traveller to God's bar, whose crime is, in being "born with a skin not coloured like his own;" and if it may inspire in the youthful mind, the spirit of that sweet verse, consecrated by the hallowed associations of a New-England home—

"I was not born a little slave
To Labour in the sun,
And wish I were but in my grave,
And all my labor done."

it will not be in vain.

That it may hasten that glorious consummation which we know is fast approaching, when slavery shall be known only in the story of past time, is the earnest prayer of the

AUTHOR.

Certificate of the Citizens of Spencertown.

This is to certify, that we, the undersigned, are, and have been *well acquainted* with Peter Wheeler, for a number of years, and that we place *full confidence in all his statements*:—

ERASTUS PRATT, Justice of the Peace.
CHARLES B. DUTCHER, do. do.
ABIAH W. MAYHEW, Deacon of the Presbyterian Church.
CHARLES H. SKIFF, M. D.
WILLIAM A. DEAN.
JOHN GROFF.
DANIEL BALDWIN.
ELISHA BABCOCK.
PHILIP STRONG.
PATRICK M. KNAPP.
WILLIAM TRAVER.
EPHRAIM BERNUS.
SAMUEL HIGGINS.
WILLIAM PARSONS.
JAMES BALDWIN.
FRANCIS CHAREVOY.

[It may be proper to state that many of these gentlemen have known Peter more than thirteen years; likewise, that they are men of the first respectability.

—Author.]

CONTENTS.

~

BOOK THE FIRST.

CHAPTER I.

CHAPTER II.

CHAPTER III.

But Capt. Truesdell promises to protect him, "as long as grass grows and water runs—He follows the river."

BOOK THE FIRST.

PETER WHEELER IN CHAINS.
DEDICATED TO

Every body who hates oppression, and don't believe that it is right, under any circumstances, to buy and sell the image of the Great God Almighty; and to all who love Human Liberty well enough to help to break every yoke, that the oppressed may go free; God bless all such!

"I own I am shocked at the *purchase* of slaves,
And fear those that buy them and sell them are knaves;
What I hear of their hardships, their tortures and groans,
Is almost enough to draw pity from stones."

COWPER.

CHAPTER I.

Author's first interview with Peter—Peter calls on the Author, and begins his story—his birth and residence—is adopted by Mrs. Mather and lives in Mr. Mather's house—his *"red scarlet coat"*—fishing expedition on Sunday with Hagar when he sees the Devil—a feat of horsemanship—saves the life of master's oldest son, and is bit in the operation by a wild hog—an encounter with an "old fashioned cat owl" in the Cedar Swamp—a man killed by wild cats—a short "sarmint" at a Quaker Meeting—"I and John makes a pincushion of a calf's nose, and got *tuned* for it, I tell ye"— holyday's amusements—the marble egg—"I and John great cronies"— Mistress sick—Peter hears something in the night which he thinks a forerunner of her death—*she dies a Christian*—her dying words—Peter's feelings on her death.

Author. "Peter, your history is so remarkable, that I have thought it would make quite an interesting book; and I have a proposal to make you."

Peter. "Well, Sir, I'm always glad to hear the Domine talk; what's your proposal? I guess you're contrivin' to put a spoke in the Abolition wheel, ain't ye?"

A. "Peter you know I'm a friend to the black man, and try to do him good."

P. "Yis, I know that, I tell ye."

A. "Well, I was going to say that this question of Slavery is all the talk every where, and as *facts* are so necessary to help men in coming to correct conclusions in regard to it, I have thought it would be a good thing to write a story of your life and adventures—for you know that every body likes to read such books, and they do a great deal of good in the cause of Freedom."

P. "I s'pose then you've got an idee of makin' out some sich a book as Charles Ball, and that has done a sight of good. But it seems to me I've *suffered* as much as Charles Ball, and I've sartinly *travelled ten times as fur* as he ever did. But *I* should look funny enough in print, shouldn't I? The Life and Adventers of Peter Wheeler—!! ha! ha!! ha!!! And then you see every feller here in town, would be a stickin' up his nose at the very idee, jist because I'm a "nigger" as they say—or "snow-ball," or somethin' else; but never mind, if it's a goin' to du any *good*, why I say *let split*, and we'll go it nose or no nose—snow-ball or no snow-ball."

A. "Well, I'm engaged this morning Peter, but if you will call down to my study this afternoon at two o'clock, I'll be at home, and ready to begin. I want you to put on your "thinking cap," and be prepared to begin your story, and I'll write while you talk, and in this way we'll do a good business—good bye Peter, give my love to your family, and be down in season."

P. "Good bye Domine, and jist give *my* love to your folks; and I'll be down afore two, if nothin' happens more'n I know on."

~

A. "Walk in—Ah! Peter you're come have you? you are *punctual* too, for the clock is just striking. I'm glad to see you; take a seat on the settee."

P. "I thought I couldn't be fur out of the way: and I'm right glad to see *you* tu, and you pretty well? and how does your lady du?"

A. "All well, Peter."

P. "You seem to be all ready to weigh anchor."

A. "Yes, and we'll be soon under way.—And now, Peter, I have perfect confidence in your veracity, but I want you to watch every word you utter, for 'twill all be read by ten thousand folks, and I wouldn't send out any ex-aggerated statement, or coloured story, for all the books in Christendom. You know it's hard to tell "the truth, the whole truth, and nothing but the truth;" and now you will have plenty of time to *think,* for I can't write as fast as you will talk, and I want you to think carefully, and speak accurately, and we'll have a *true* story, and I think a *good* one."

P. "I'll take good care of that, Mr. L—and we'll have a *true* story if we don't have a big one; but I'm a thinkin' that afore we git through we'll have a pretty good yarn spun, as the sailors say. I always thought 'twas bad enough to tell one lie, but a man must be pretty bad to tell one in a book, for if he has ten thousand books printed, he will print ten thousand lies, and that's lying on tu big a scale."

A. "Well, Peter, in what age, and quarter of the world were you born?"

P. "As near as I can find out, I was born the 1st of January 1789, at Little Egg Harbour, a parish of Tuckertown, New Jersey. I was born a slave— and many a time, like old Job, I've *cussed* the day I was born. My mother has often told me, that my great grandfather was born in Africa, and one day he and his little sister was by the seaside pickin' up shells, and there come a small boat along shore with white sailors, and ketches 'em both, and they cried to go back and see mother, but they didn't let 'em go, and they look 'em off to a big black ship that was crowded with negroes they'd stole; and there they kept 'em in a dark hole, and almost starved and choked for some weeks, they should guess, and finally landed 'em in Baltimore, and there they was *sold.* Grandfather used to set and tell these 'ere stories all over to mother, and set and cry and cry jist like a child, arter he'd got to be an old man, and tell how he wanted to see mother on board that ship, and how happy he and his sister was, a playing in the sand afore the ship come; and jist so mother used to set and trot me on her knee, and tell me these 'ere stories as soon as I could understand 'em—"

"Well, as I was sayin', I was born in Tuckertown, and my master's name was Job Mather. He was a man of family and property, and had a wife and two sons, and a large plantation. He was a Quaker by profession, and used to go to the Quaker meetin's; but afore I git through with him, I'll show you he warn't overstocked with Religion. He was the first and last Quaker I ever heard on, that owned a slave,[i] and he warn't a *full-blooded Quaker,* for if he had been, he wouldn't owned me; for a full-blooded Quaker won't own a slave. I was the only slave he owned, and he didn't own me but this, is the way he *come by* me.[ii] Mistress happened to have a child the same time I was born, and the littler feller died. So she sent to Dinah my mother, and got me to nuss her, when I was only eight days old."

"Well, arter I'd got weaned, and was about a year old, mother comes to mistress, and says she, 'Mistress, have you got through with my baby?' 'No,' says Mistress, 'no Dinah, I mean to bring him up myself.' And so she kept me, and called me Peter Wheeler, for that was my father's name, and so I lived in master's family almost jist like his own children."

"The first thing I recollect was this:—Master and Mistress, went off up country on a journey, and left I and John, (John was her little boy almost my age,) with me at home, and says she as she goes away, now boys if you'll be *good,* when I come back, I'll bring you some handsome presents."

"Well, we *was* good, and when she comes back, she gives up both a suit of clothes, and mine was *red scarlet,* and it had a little coat buttoned on to a pair of trousers, and a good many buttons on 'em, all up and down befor'ard and behind, and I had a little cap, with a good long tostle on it; and oh! when I first got 'em on, if I didn't feel *big,* I won't guess."

"I used to do 'bout as I was a mind tu, until I was eight or nine year old, though Master and Mistress used to make I and John keep Sunday *'mazin strict;* yet, I remember one Sunday, when they was gone to Quaker-meetin', I and Hagar, (she was my sister, and lived with my mother, and mother was free,) well, I and Hagar went down to the creek jist by the house, a fishin'. *She* stood on the bridge, and *I* waded out up to my middle, and had big luck, and in an hour I had a fine basket full. But jist then I see a flouncin' in the water, and a great monstrous big thing got hold of my hook, and yauked it arter him, pole, line, nigger and all, I'd enemost said, and if he didn't make a squashin' then I'm a white man. Well, Hagar see it, and she was scart almost to pieces, and off she put for the house, and left me there alone. Well, I thought sure 'nough 'twas the Devil, I'd hearn tell so much 'bout the old feller'; and I took my basket and put out for the house like a white-head, and I thought I *should* die, I was *so scart.* We got to the house and hid under the bed, all a tremblin' jist like a leaf, afeard to stir one inch. Pretty soon the old folks comes home, and so out we crawled, and they axed us the matter, and so we up and telled 'em all about it, and Master, says he 'why sure 'nough 'twas the Devil, and all cause you went a fishin' on a Sunday, and if you go down there a fishin' agin Sunday he'll catch you both, and that'll be the eend of you two snowballs."

A. "Didn't he whip you, Peter, to pay for it?"

P. "Whip us? No, Sir; I tell ye what 'tis what he telled us 'bout the Devil, paid us more'n all the whippens in creation."

A. "What was the big thing in the creek?"

P. "Why, I s'pose 'twas a *shark;* they used to come up the creek from the ocean."

A. "Did you have much Religious Intruction?"

P. "Why, the old folks used to tell us we musn't lie and steal and play Sabbaday, for if we did, the *old boy* would come and carry us off; and that was 'bout all the Religion I got from them, and all I knowed 'bout it, as long as I lived there."

A. "What did you used to do when you got old enough to work?"

P. "Why, I lived in the house, and almost jist like a gal I knew when washin'-day come, and I'd out with the poundin'-barrel, and *on* with the big kittle, and besides I used to do all the heavy cookin' in the kitchen, and carry the dinner out to the field hands, and scrub, and scour knives, and all sich work."

A. "Did you always used to have plenty to eat?"

P. Oh? yis, Sir, I had the handlin' of the victuals, and I had my *fill,* I tell ye."

A. "Did you ever go to school, Peter?"

P. "Yis, Sir, I went one day when John was sick in his place, and that was the only day I ever went, in all my life, and I larned my A, B, C's through, both ways, and never forgot 'em arter that."

A. "Well, did you ever meet with any accidents?"

P. "Why, it's a wonder I'm *alive,* I've had so many wonderful *escapes.* When I was 'bout ten year old, Master had a beautiful horse, only he was as wild as a painter, and so one day when he was gone away, I and John gits him out, and he puts me on, and ties my legs under his belly, so I shouldn't git flung off, and he ran, and snorted, and broke the string, and pitched me off, and enemost broke my head, and if my skull hadn't a been pretty thick, I guess he would; and I didn't get well in almost six weeks." Another thing I think on, Master had some of these 'ere old-fashioned long-eared and long-legged hogs, and he used to turn 'em out, like other folks, in a big wood near by, and when they was growed up, fetch 'em and pen 'em up, and fat 'em; and so Master fetched home two that was dreadful wild, and they had tushes *so long,* and put 'em in a pen to fat. Well, his oldest son gits over in the pen one day to clean out the trough, and one on 'em put arter him, and oh! how he *bawled,* and run to git out; I heard him, and run and reached over the pen, and catched hold on him, and tried to lift him out; but the old feller had got hold of his leg, and took out a whole mouthful, and then let go; and I pulled like a good feller, and got him most over, but the old sarpent got hold of *my hand,* and bit it through and through, and there's the scar yit."

A. "Did you let go, Peter?"

P. "Let go? No! I tell ye I didn't; the hog got hold of his heel, and bit the ball right off; but when he let go *that* time, I fetched a dreadful lift, and I got him over the pen, *safe and sound, only* he was badly bit."

"And while I think of it, one day Mistress took me to go with her through the Cedar Swamp to see some 'lations, only she took me as she said to keep the snakes off. It was two miles through the woods, and we went on a road of cedar-rails, and when we got into the swamp, I see a big old-fashioned cat-owl a settin' on a limb up 'bout fifteen foot from the ground I guess; and as I'd heard an owl couldn't see in the day-time, I thought I'd creep up slily, and catch him, and I says 'Mistress,' says I, 'will you wait?' and she says, 'yis, if you'll be quick." And so up I got, and jist as I was agoin to grab him, he jumped down, and lit on my head, and planted his big claws in my wool and begun to peck, and I hollered like a loon, and swung off, and down I come, and he stuck tight and pecked worse than ever. I hollows for Mistress, and by this time she comes up with a club, and she pounded the old feller, but he wouldn't git off, and she pounded him till he was dead; and his claws stuck so tight in my wool, Mistress, had to cut 'em out with my jack-knife, and up I got, glad 'nough to git off as I did; and I crawled out of the mud, and the blood come a runnin' down my head, and I was clawed and pecked like a good feller, but I didn't go owlin' agin very soon, I tell ye."

"Well, we got there, and this was Saturday, and we stayed till the next arternoon. Sunday mornin' I see a man go by, towards our house, with an axe on his shoulder; and we started in the arternoon, and when we'd got into the middle of the swamp there lay that man *dead,* with two big wild cats by him that he'd killed: he'd split one on 'em open in the head, and the axe lay buried in the neck of t'other; and there they all lay dead together, all covered with blood, and sich a pitiful sight I hain't seen. But oh! how thick the wild cats was in that swamp, and you could hear 'em squall in the night, as thick as frogs in the spring; but ginerally they kept pretty still in the day time, and so we didn't think there was any danger till now; and we had to leave the dead man there alone, only the dead wild cats was with him, and make tracks as fast as we cleverly could, for home."

A. "Did you ever go to meetings?"

P. "Sometimes I used to go to Quaker meetin's with mistress, and there we'd set and look first at one and then at t'other; and bi'm'by somebody would up and say a word or two, and down he'd set, and then another, and *down he'd set.* Sometimes they was the stillest, and sometimes the noisiest meetin's I ever see. One time, I remember, we went to hear a new Quaker preacher, and there was a mighty sight of folks there; and I guess we set still an hour, without hearin' a word from anybody: and that'ere feller was a waitin' for *his spirit,* I s'pose; and, finally at last, an old woman gits up and squarks through her nose, and says she, "Oh! all you young gentlemen beware of them 'ere young ladies—Ahem!—Oh! all you young ladies beware of them 'ere young gentlemen—Ahem—Peneroyal tea is good for a cold! and down she sat, and I roared right out, and I never was so tickled in all my life; and the rest on 'em looked as sober as setten' hens:—but I couldn't hold in, and I snorted out *straight;* and so mistress wouldn't let me go agin. And now you are a Domine, and I wants to ask you if the Lord inspired her to git up, whether or no He didn't forsake her soon arter she *got* up?"

A. "Why, Peter, you've made the same remark about her, that a famous historian makes about Charles Second, a wicked king of England. Some of the king's friends said, the Grace of God brought him to the throne—this historian said, "if it *brought* him to the throne it forsook him very soon after he *got* there."

A. "Did you have any fun holydays, Peter."

P. "Oh! yis, I and John used to be 'mazing thick, and always together, and always in mischief—One time, I recollect, when master was gone away, we cut up a curious dido; master had a calf that was dreadful gentle, and I and John takes him, and puts a rope round his neck, and pulls his nose through the fence, and drove it full of pins, and he blatted and blat-ted like murder, and finally mistress see us, and out she come, and makes us pull all the pins out, one by one, and let him go; she didn't say much, but goes and cuts a parcel of sprouts, and I concluded she was a goin' to *tune* us. But it come night, we went into the house, and she was mighty good, and says she, 'come boys, I guess it's about bed time;' and so she hands us a couple of basins of samp and milk, and we eat it, and off to bed, a chuck-lin', to think we'd got off as well as we had. But we'd no sooner got well to bed, and nicely kivered up, when I see a light comin' up stairs, and mistress was a holdin' the candle in one hand, and a bunch of sprouts in the t'other; and she comes up to the bed, and says she, 'boys do you sleep warm? I guess I'll tuck you up a little warmer, and, at that, she off with every rag of bed clothes, and if she *didn't tune* us, I miss my guess: and 'now,' says she, 'John see that you be in better business next time, when your dad's gone; and *you nigger*, you good for nothin little rascal, you make a pincushion of a calf's nose agin,' will ye?' And I tell ye they *set close, them 'ere sprouts.*"

A. "Well, Peter, you were going to talk about holydays, and I shouldn't think it much of a holyday to be 'tuned with them sprouts.'"

P. "Oh! yis, Sir, we had great times every Christmas and New-Years; but we thought the most of Saint Valentine's Day. The boys and gals of the whole neighborhood, used to git together, and carry one, and make fun, and *sich like.* We used to play pin a good deal, and I and John used to go snacks, and cheat like Sancho Panza; and there's where we got the pins to stick in the calf's nose, I was tellin' you on. We used to have a good deal of *fun* sometimes in *bilein eggs.* Mistress would send us out to hunt eggs, and we'd find a nest of a dozen, likely, and only carry in three or four, and lay the rest by for holydays. Well, we used to bile eggs, as I was sayin', and the boys would strike biled eggs together, and the one that didn't get his egg broke should have t'other's, for his'n was the best egg. Well, we got a contrivance, I and John did, that brought us a fine bunch of eggs. John's uncle was down the country once, and he gin John a smooth marble egg: oh! 'twas a dreadful funny thing, and I guess he's got it yit, if he's a livin'— well, we kept this egg, year in, and year out, and we'd take it to the holy-days, and break all the eggs there, and carry home a nice parcel, and have a good bunch to give away, and I guess as how the boys never found it out."

A. "Why, you had as good times as you could ask for, it seems to me."

P. "Oh! yis, Sir, I see many bright days, and, when I was a boy, I guess no feller had more fun than I did. And I mean, Domine, all through the book, to tell things jist as they was, and when I was frolicsome and happy I'll say so, and when I was in distress, I'll say so; for it seems to me, a book ought to tell things jist as they be. Well, I had got about to the eend of my happy fun, for mistress, who was the best friend I had, was took sick, and I expected her to die—and sure 'nough she did die; and as I was kind 'a superstitious, one night afore she died, I heard some strange noises, that scart me, and made me think 'em forerunners of mistress' death; and for years and years them noises used to trouble me distressedly. Well, mistress had been a good woman, and died *like a christian.* When she thought she was a dyin', she called up her husband to her bed-side, and took him by the hand, and says, 'I am now goin' to my God, and your God, and I want you to prepare to follow me to heaven,' and says, 'farewell;' she puts her arms round his neck and kisses him. Then she calls up her children, and says pretty much the same thing to them; and then me, and she puts her arms round all our necks, and kisses us all, and says 'good bye dear children,' and she fell back into the bed and died, without a struggle or a groan.

Oh! how I cried when mistress died. She had been kind to me and loved me, and it seemed I hadn't any thing left in the world worth livin' for; put it all together, I guess I cried more'n a week 'bout it, and nothin' would pacify me. I *loved* mistress, and when I see her laid in the grave it broke my heart. I have never in all my life with all my sufferin's had any affliction that broke me down as that did. I thought I *should* die: the world looked gloomy 'round me, and I knew I had nothin' to expect from master after she was gone, and I was left in the world friendless and alone. I had seen *some,* yis *many,* good days, and I don't believe on arth there was a happier boy than Peter Wheeler; but when mistress closed her eyes in death, my sorrows begun; and oh! the tale of 'em will make your heart ache, afore I finish, for all my hopes, and all my fun, and all my happiness, was buried in mistress' grave."

A. "Well, Peter, I'm tired of writing, and suppose we adjourn till tomorrow."

P. "Well, Sir, that'll do I guess—oh! afore I go, have you got any more 'Friend of Man?"

A. "Oh! yes, and something better yet—here's Thomson and Breckenridge's Debate."

P. "Is that the same Thomson that the slavery folks drove out of the country, and the gentleman of property and standing in Boston tried to tar and feather?"

A. ""YES."

P. "Well, I reckon he must have rowed Breckenridge up Salt River."

A. "You're right, Peter, and he left him on Dry Dock!!!"
P. "Good bye, Domine."
A. "Good bye, Peter."

ENDNOTES FOR CHAPTER I

i. Would to God, it could be said of any other denomination of Christians in Christendom!!

ii. A grand distinction for some *big Doctors* to learn!

CHAPTER II.

Peter emancipated by his old Master's Will—but is stolen and sold at auction, and bid off by GIDEON MOREHOUSE—Hagar tries to buy her brother back—parting scene—his reception at his new Master's—sudden change in fortune—Master's cruelty—the Muskrat skins—prepare to go into "the new countries"—start on the journey "incidents of travel" on the road—Mr. Sterling, who is a sterling-good man, tries to buy Peter—gives him a pocket full of "Bungtown coppers"—abuse—story of the Blue Mountain—Oswego—Mr. Cooper, an Abolitionist—journey's end—Cayuga county, New York.

Author. "Well, Peter, I've come up to your house this morning, to write another chapter in the book; and you can go on with your boots while I write, and so we'll kill two birds with one stone."

Peter. "Well, I felt distressedly when mistress died, and I cried, and mourned, and wept, night and day. I was now in my eleventh year. While she lived I worked in the house, but, as soon as she died, I was put into the field; and so, on her death, I entered into what I call the field of trouble; and now my story will show ye what stuff men and women is made of.

"My master didn't *own* me, for I was made free by my old master's *will*, who died when I was *little;* and, in his will, he liberated my mother, who had always been a slave and all her posterity; so that as soon as old master died, I *was free by law—but pity me if slavery folks regard law that ever I see:* for slavery is a tramplin' on all laws. Well, arter mother was free, she got a comfortable livin' till her death. In that will I was set free, but I lived with master till after mistress' death, and then I was *stole,* and in this way. Master got uneasy and thought he could do better than to stay in that country, and so he advertised his plantation for sale. It run somethin' like this, on the notice he writ:

'FOR SALE,
'A plantation well stocked with oxen, horses, sheep, hogs, fowls, &c.—and one young, smart nigger, sound every way.

"You see they put me on the stock-list!! Well, when the day came that I was to be sold, oh! how I felt! I knew it warn't *right,* but what could *I* do? *I was a black boy.* They sold one thing, and then another, and bim'bye they made me mount a table, and then the auctioneer cries out:

'Here's a smart, active, sound, well trained, young nigger—he's a first rate body servant, good cook, and all that; now give us a *bid.*' and one man bid $50, and another $60; and so they went on. Sister Hagar, she was four years older than me, come up and got on to the table with me, (they dassent sell her,) and she began to cry, and sob, and pity me, and says she, 'oh, Peter, you ain't agoin' way off, be ye, 'mong the wild Ingens at the west, be ye?' You see there was some talk, that a man would buy me, who was a goin' out into York State, and you know there was a *sight* of Ingens here then, and folks was as 'fraid to go to York State then, as they be now to go to Texas—and so Hagar put her arms round my neck, and oh! how she cried; $95 cries out one man; $100 cries another, and so they kept bidden' while Hagar and I kept a cryin' and finally, GIDEON MOREHOUSE (oh! it fairly makes my blood run cold, to speak that name, to this day,) well, he bid $110, and took me—master made him promise to school me three quarters, or he'd not give him a bill of sale; so he promised to do it, and I was his Property. And that's all a slaveholder's word is good for, for he never sent me to school a day in his life. Now, how could that man get any *right* to me, when he bought me as *stolen property;* or how could any body have even a *legal right* to me? why no more as I see than you would have to my cow, if you should buy her of a man that stole her out of my barn. And yit that's the way that every slaveholder gits his right to every slave, for a body must know that a feller *owns himself.* But I gin up long ago all idee of slavery folks thinkin' any thing 'bout *law.*

"Well, I should think I stood on that table two hours, for I know when I come down, my eyes ached with cryin' and my legs with standin' and tears run down my feet, and fairly made a puddle there. Sister Hagar, she was a very lovin' sister, and she felt distressedly to think her brother was a goin' to be sold; and so she went round and borrowed and begged all the money she could, and that, with what she had afore, made 110 Mexican dollars, jist what I sold for, and she comes to my new master, and says she, 'Sir, I've got $110 to buy my brother back agin, and I don't want him to go off to the west, and wont you please Sir, be so kind, as sell me back my brother?' 'Away with ye,' he hollered, 'I'll not take short of 150 silver dollars, and bring me that or nothin';' and so Hagar tried hard to raise so much, but she couldn't, and oh! how she cried, and come to me and sobbed, and hung round my neck, and took on dreadfully, and wouldn't be pacified; and besides, mother stood by, and see it all, and felt distressedly, as you know a mother must; but, what could *she* do? she was a *black woman.* Now, how would your mother feel to see you sold into bondage? Why, arter mistress died, it did seem to me that master become *a very devil*—he 'bused me and other folks most all-killin'ly. He married a fine gal as soon arter mistress' death as she would have him; and she had 400 silver dollars, and a good many other things, and he took her money and went off to Philadelphia, and sold some of his property, and the rest at this auction I tell on; and then told her she must leave the premises, and another man come on to 'em, and she had to go; and she and Hagar lived together a good many year, and got their livin' by spinnin' and weavin', and she was *almost* broken hearted all the time; and when I got way off into the new countries, I hears from Hagar, that she died *clear* broken hearted. Well, I was sold a Friday, and master was to take me to Morehouse's a Sunday; Sunday come, and I was *obliged* to go. I parted from mother, and never see her agin, till I heard she was dead; but you must know how I felt, so I won't describe it. She felt distressedly, and gin me a good deal of good advice, but oh! t'was a sorrowful day for our little family, I tell ye, Mr. L—.

Well, I got to my new master's, and all was mighty good, and the children says, "Oh! dis black boy fader bought, and he shall sleep with me;" and the children most worshipped me, and mistress gin me a great hunk of gingerbread, and I thought I had the nicest place in the world. But my joy was soon turned into sorrow. I slept that night on a straw bed, and nothin' but an old ragged coverlid over me; and next morning I didn't go down to make a fire, for old master always used to do that himself; and so when I comes down, master scolds at me, and boxes my ears pretty hard, and says, 'I didn't buy you to play the gentleman, you black son of a bitch—I got ye to work.'

"Well, I began to grow home-sick; and when he was cross and abusive, I used to think of mistress.

"Master was a cabinet-maker; and so next day, says he, 'I'm agoin' to make you larn the trade,' and he sets me to planin' rough cherry boards; and when it come night, my arms was so lame I couldn't lift 'em to my head, pushin' the jack-plane; and he kept me at this cabinet work till the first day of May, when I got so I could make a pretty decent bedstead. I come to live with him the first of March, and now he begins to fix and git ready for to move out to the new countries. Well, when we was a packin' up the tools, I happened to hit a chisel agin' a hammer, and dull it a little, and he gets mad, and cuffs me, and thrashes me 'bout the shop, and swears like a pirate. I says, 'Master, I sartinly didn't mean to do it.' 'You lie, you black devil, you did,' he says; 'and if you say another word, I'll split your head open with the broad-axe.' Well, *I felt bad 'nough,* but said nothin'. He advertised all his property pretty much, and sold it at vandue; and now we was nearly ready for a start. Master had promised to let me go and see sister Hagar, and mother, a few days afore we started; and as he was gone, mistress told me I might go. So I had liberty, and I detarmined to use it. I had catched six large muskrats, and had the skins, and thinks I to myself, what's mine is *my own;* and so I up stairs, and wraps a paper round 'em, and flings 'em out the window, and puts out with them for town, and sold 'em for a quarter of a dollar a piece. I went Friday; but I didn't see mother, for she was gone away, and Sunday I spent visiting Hagar, and that night I got home. While I was gone they had found out the skins was a missin'; and soon as I'd got home, I see somethin' was to pay; for master looked dreadful *wrothy* when I come in, and none of the family said a word, 'how de,' nor nothing, only Lecta, one of the gals, asked me how the folks did, and if I had a good visit; and she kept a talkin', and finally, the old lady kind a scowled at her, (you see the muskrat skins set hard on her stomach,) and finally, master looked at me cross enough to turn milk sour, and says he, 'Nigger, do you know anything 'bout them skins?' Says I, 'No, Sir;' and I lied, it's true, but I was *scart.* And says he, 'you lie, you black devil.' So I stuck to it, and kept a stickin' to it, and he kept a growing madder, and says he, 'If you don't own it, I'll whip your guts out.' So he goes and gits a long whip and bed-cord, and that scart me worser yit, and I *had to own it,* and I confessed I had the money I got for 'em, all but a sixpence I had spent for gingerbread; and he searched my pocket, and took it all away, and *half a dollar besides, that Mary Brown gin me to remember her by!!*—and then he gin me five or six cuts over the head, and says he, 'Now, you dam nigger, if I catch you in another such lie, I'll cut your dam hide off on ye;' and then he drives me off to bed, without any supper; and he says, 'If you ain't down *airly* to make a fire, I'll be up arter ye with a raw hide.'

"Well, next day we went to fixin' two kivered wagons for the journey; and, arter we'd got all fixed to start, he sends me over to his mother's to shell some seed corn, up stairs, in a tub. Well, I hadn't slept 'nough long back, and so, in spite of my teeth, I got to sleep in the tub. He comes over there, and finds me asleep in the tub, and he takes up a flail staff and hits me over the head, and cussed and swore, and telled his mother to see I didn't git to sleep, nor have anything to eat in all day. Well, arter he'd gone, the old lady called me down, and gin me a good fat meal, and telled me to go up and shell corn as fast as I could. Well, I did, and it come night—I got a good supper, and put out for home; and I've always found the women cleverer than the men—they're kind'a tender-hearted, ye know.

"Well, we got ready, and off we started, and I guess 'twas the 9th of May; and I drove a team of four horses, and it had the *chist* of tools and family; and he drove another team, full of other things, and his brother-in-law, Mr. Abers, who was agoin' out to larn the trade; and Abers was mighty good to me.

"Well, we started for York State, and one night we stayed in Newark, and I thought 'twas a dreadful handsome place; for you could see New York and Brooklyn from there, and the waters round New York, that's the handsomest waters I ever see, and I have seen hundreds of harbors.

"Next day we got to a place called Long Cummin, and put up at a Mr. Starling's, and he kept a store and tavern, and they was fine folks. In the evenin' Mr. Starling comes into the kitchen where I was a sittin' by the fire, holdin' one of the children in my lap, and he slaps me on the shoulder, and master comes in too, and says he, 'Morehouse, what will you take for that boy, cash down? I want him for the store and tavern, and run arrants, &c.' Master says, 'I don't want to sell him.'—'Well,' says Starling, 'I'll give you $200 cash in hand.' Master says, 'I wouldn't take 500 silver dollars for that boy, for I mean to have the workin' of that nigger myself.' 'Well,' says Starling, 'you'd better take that, or you won't git anything, for he'll be running off bim'bye.' And I tell ye, I begun to think 'bout it myself, about that time. Well, I went to bed, and thought about it, and wanted to stay with Starling; and next mornin' Mrs. Starling comes to master, and says she, 'I guess you'd better sell that boy to my husband for he's jist the boy we want to git:' and says I, 'Master, I wants to stay here, and I wish you'd sell me to these 'ere folks;'—and with that he up and kicked me, and says he, 'If I hear any more of that from *you*, I'll tie ye up, and tan your black hide; and now go, and up with the teams.' Well, when we got all ready to start, I wanted to stay, and I boohooed and boohooed; and Mr. Starling says to master, 'I want your boy to come in the store a minute;' and I went in, and he out with a bag of Bungtown coppers, and gin me a hull pocket full, and says he, 'Peter, I wish you could live with me, but you can't; and you must be a good boy, and when you git to be a man you'll see better times, I hope;' and I cried, and took on dreadfully, and bellowed jist like a bull; for you know, when a body's grieved, it makes a body feel a good deal worse to have a body pity 'em. I see there was no hope, and I mounted the box, and took the lines, and driv off; but I felt as bad as though I had been goin' to my funeral. Oh! it seemed to me they was all happy there, and they was so kind to me, and they seemed to be so good, it almost broke my heart: I had every thing to eat—broiled shad, cake, apple pie, (I used to be a great hand for apple pie,) rice pudden' and raisins in it, beefsteak, and all that; and the children kept a runnin' round the table, and sayin', 'Peter must have this, and Peter must have that;' and I kept a thinkin' as I drove on, how they all kept flocking round me when we come away, and I cried 'bout it two or three days, and every time master come up, he'd give me a lick over my ears, 'cause I was a cryin'. If I should die I couldn't think of the next place where we stayed all night. We travelled thirty miles, and the tavern keeper's name was Henry Williams. Well, the day arter, we had a very steep hill to go down, and the leaders run on fast, and I couldn't hold 'em, and when we got to the bottom, master hollered, 'Stop!' and up he come, and *whipped me dreadfully,* and *kicked me with a pair of heavy boots* so hard in my back, I was so lame I couldn't hardly walk for three or four days, and every body asked what was the matter. The next place we stopped at, the tavern keeper's folks was old, and real clever; and master told 'em not to let me have any supper but buttermilk, and that set me to cryin', and I boohooed a considerable; and the darter says, 'Come, mother, let's give Peter a good supper, and his master will pay for it, tu;' and so they did; and as I was a settin' by the fire, she axed me, and I told her all 'bout how I was treated, and says she, 'Why don't you run away, Peter? I wouldn't stay with sich a man: I'd run, if I had to stay in the woods.' Next mornin' the old man was mad 'nough when he see the bill for my buttermilk, and swore a good deal 'bout it. Next day we come to the 'Beach Woods,' and 'twas the roughest road you ever see, and the wheels would go down in the mud up to the hubs, then up on a log; and he'd make me lift the wheels as hard as I any way could, and he wouldn't lift a pound, and stood over me with his whip, and sung out, *'lift, you black devil, lift.'* And I did lift, till I could fairly see stars, and go back and forth from one wagon to t'other, he to whip, and I to lift; and so we kept a tuggin' through the day till night. That night we stayed to a *black man's tavern;* and when we come up, and see 'twas a black man's house, master was mad 'nough; but he couldn't git any furder that night, and so he had to be an abolitionist once in his life, any how!!! Well, he didn't drive that nigger round, I tell ye, he was on tu good footin': he owned a farm, and fine house, and we had as good fare there as any where on the road.

The next day the goin' was so bad we couldn't git out of the woods, and we had to stay there all night; and oh! what times we *did* see; I lifted and strained till I *was* dead: and that night we slept in the wagons—the women took possession of one, and we of t'other; and the woods was alive with wolves and panthers; and such a howlin' and screamin' you never heard;

but we builds up a large fire, and that kept 'em off. We lay on our faces in the wagon, with our rifles loaded, cocked and primed; and when them 'ere varmints howled, the horses trembled so the harnesses fairly shook on 'em: but there warn't any more sleep there that night, than there would be in that fire.

"Next day we worried through, and stopped at a house, and got some breakfast of bears' meat and hasty pudden'; and it come night, we made the 'Blue Mountain;' and on the top of it was some good folks; we stayed there one night, and Mr. Cooper, the landlord, come out to the barn, and axed me if I was *hired* out to that man, or *belonged* to him? 'Well,' said he, 'if you did but know it, you are free now, for you are in a free state, and it's agin' the law to bring a slave from another state into this; and where be you goin'?' 'To Cayuga County,' says I. 'Well, when you git there, du you show him your backsides, and tell him to help himself.'

The next night we stayed in Owego; but I'm afore my story, for goin' down the Blue Mountain next day, the leaders run, and I couldn't hold 'em if I should be shot, and they broke one arm off of the block tongue. Well, when I stopped, and master comes runnin' up, and he fell on, and struck me, and mauled me most awfully; and jist then a man come up on horseback, and says he to master, 'If you want to *kill* that boy, why don't ye beat his brains out with an axe and done with it—but don't maul him so; for *you* know, and *I* know, for I see it all myself, that that boy ain't able to hold that team, and I shouldn't a thought it strange if they had dashed every thing to pieces.' Well, master was mad 'nough, for that was a dreadful rebuke; and says he, 'You'd better make off with yourself, and mind your own business.' The man says, 'I don't mean to quarrel with you, and I won't; but I think ye act more like a *devil* than a *man!* So off he went; and *I love that man yit!*

Next night we stayed in Owego; and the tavern keeper, a fine man, had a talk with me arter bed-time; and says he, 'Peter, your master can't touch a hair of your head, and if you want to be free you can, for we've tried that experiment here lately; and we've got a good many slaves free in this way, and they're doing well. But if you want to run away, why *run;* but wait awhile, for you are a boy yit, and *there are folks in* York State, mean 'nough to catch you and send you back to your master!'[i]

"Well, I parted from that man, and I resolved that I would run away, but take his advice, and not run till I could clear the coop for good. Well, we finally got to the end of our journey, and put up at Henry Ludlow's house, in Milton township, and county of Cayuga, and State of New York."

A. "Well, Peter, I think we can afford to stop writing now, for I'm fairly tired out. Good bye, Peter."

P. "Good bye, Domine."

~

As I came away from the lowly cottage of Peter Wheeler, and thought of the toils and barbarities of a life of slavery, and returned to the sweet and endearing charities of my own quiet home, tenderness subdued my spirit; and I could not but repeat, with emotions of the deepest gratitude, those sweet lines of my childhood:

'I was not born a little slave,
To labor in the sun;
And wish I were but in my grave,
And all my labor done.'

Oh! I exclaimed as I entered my study, and sat down before a bright, cheerful fireside, and was greeted with the kind look of an affectionate wife, as the storm howled over the mountains, Oh! God made man to be *free,* and he must be a *wretch,* and not a man, who can quench all this social light forever. I hate slavery so much for its fetters, and whips, and starvation, as for the blight and mildew it casts upon the social and moral condition of man. Oh! enslave not a soul—a deathless spirit—trample not upon a mind, 'tis an *immortal thing.* Man perchance may light anew the torch he quenches, but the soul! Oh! tremble and beware—lay not rude hands upon God's image there—I thought of the vast territory that stretches from the Atlantic to the foot of the Rocky Mountains, and from our Southern border to the heart of our Capitol, as one mighty altar of Mammon— where so much social light is sacrificed and blotted from the universe; where so many deathless spirits, that God made free as the mountain wild bird, are chained down forever, and I kneeled around my family altar, and I could not help uttering a prayer from the depths of my soul, for the millions of *God's creatures, and my brethren,* who pass lives of loneliness and sorrow in a world which has been lighted up with the Redeemer's salvation. What a scene for man to look at when he prays: A God who loves to make all his creatures happy! A world which groans because man is a sinner! A man who loves to make his brother wretched! Oh! thought I, if prayer can reach a father's ear to night, one yoke shall be broken, and one oppressed slave shall go free.

ENDNOTE FOR CHAPTER II

i. Yes, and there are folks, yes judges and dough faced politicians enough in *the state now* who would blast all the hopes that led a poor slave on from his chains; and when he was just stepping across the threshold of the temple of freedom, dash him to degradation and slavery, and pollute that threshold with his blood. Until a fugitive from tyranny shall be safe in the asylum of the oppressed and the home of liberty, let us not be told to go to the south. And who are the men who would, who *have* done this? Certainly not *philanthropists;* for the philanthropist loves to make his brother man happy, and will always *strike* for his freedom. Certainly not *Christians;* for it was one of the most explicit enactments of God, when he established his theocracy upon earth, and incorporated into the code of his government, that "Thou shalt not deliver unto his master the servant that is escaped from his master unto thee." (Deut. xxii, 15.) And can a man, who respects and regards the laws of heaven, turn traitor to God, and prostrate, at one fell swoop, all the claims of benevolence the fugitive slave imposes, when he lifts his fetter-galled arms to his brother, and cries, "Oh! help me to freedom—to liberty—to heaven?"

CHAPTER III.

They get into a wild country, "full of all kinds of varmints," and begin to build—Peter knocked off of a barn by his master—story of a rattle-snake charming a child—Peter hews the timber for a new house, and gets paid in lashes—Tora Ludlow an abolitionist—Peter's friends all advise him to run off—the fox-tail company, their expeditions on Oneida Lake—deer stories—Rotterdam folks—story of a painter—master pockets Peter's share of the booty and bounty—the girls of the family befriend him—a sail on the Lake—Peter is captain, and saves the life of a young lady who falls overboard, and nearly loses his own—kindly and generously treated by the young lady's father, who gives Peter a splendid suit of clothes worth seventy dollars, and "a good many other notions"—his master steals his clothes and wears them out himself—Mr. Tucker's opinion of his character, and Peter's of his fate.

Author. "Well, Peter, you found yourself in a wild country, out there in Cayuga, I reckon."

Peter. "You're right, there's no mistake 'bout *that;* most every body lived in log houses, and the woods was full of wild varmints as they could hold; well, as soon as we'd got there, we went to buildin' a log house; for see master owned a large farm out there, and as soon as we gits there we goes right on to work; we finally got the house up, and gits into it, and durin' the time I suffered *most unaccountably.* There we went to buildin' a log barn tu, and we had to notch the logs at both ends to fay into each other; well, as I was workin' on 'em, I got one notched, and we lifted it up breast high to put it on, and he sees 'twas a *leetle* tu short, and nobody was to blame, and if any body 'twas *him,* for he measured it off; but he no sooner sees it, than he drops his eend, and doubles up his fist, and knockes me on the temples, while I was yit a holdin' on, and down I went, and the log on me, and oh! how he *swore!* well, it struck my foot, and smashed it as flat as a pancake, and in five minutes it swelled up as big as a puffball, and I couldn't hardly walk for a week, and yit I had to be on the move all the time, and he *cussed* cause I didn't go faster. When I gits up I couldn't only stand on one leg, but he made me stand on it, and lift up that log breast high, but he didn't lift a pound, but cried out, '*lift, lift,* you black cuss.' Well, we got the logs up, and when we was a puttin' the rafters on, I happened to make a mistake in not gittin' one on 'em into the right place, and he knocked me off of the plate, where I was a standin' and I and the rafter went a tumblin' together, down to the ground. It hurt me distressedly, and I cried, but gits up, and says, 'master, I thinks you treat me rather.' 'Stop your mouth, you black devil, or I'll throw these 'ere adz at your head;' and I *had* to shet my mouth, *pretty sudden, tu,* and keep it shet, and he made me lift up that rafter when I couldn't hardly stand, and keep on to work; and there I set on the evesplate a tremblin' jist like a leaf, and every move he made, I 'spected he'd hurl me off 'agin', and his voice seemed like a tempest—oh! how savage! But he didn't knock me *off* agin'—I had to thatch that barn in the coldest kind of weather, with nothin' but ragged thin clothes on; and I used to git some bloody floggin's, cause I didn't thatch fast enough.

"But I've talked long 'nough 'bout him, and jist for amusement, I'm a goin' to tell ye a story 'bout a rattlesnake, and you may put it in the book, or not, jist as ye like.

"We lived, as I was a tellin', in a dreadful wild country, and 'twas full of all kinds of wild varmints—wolves, and panthers, and bears, was 'mazing plenty, and rattlesnakes mighty thick; and so one day, as we comes into dinner, mistress seemed to be rather out of humor, and she sets the baby down on the floor in a pet, and he crawls under the bed, and begins to be very full of play. He'd laugh, and stick his little hands out, and draw 'em back, and, as my place in the summer was generally on the outside door, on the sill, I happened to look under the bed, and there I see a bouncin' bit rattlesnake, stickin' his head up through a big crack, and as the child draws his hands back, the snake sticks his head up agin'. I sings out, with a loud voice, and says I, 'master, there's a rattlesnake under the bed.' 'You lie,' says he; and says I, 'why master, only jist look for yourself," and, at that, mistress runs to the bed, and snatches up the baby, and it screamed and cried, and there was no way of pacifyin' on it in the world. Well, master begins to think I speaks the truth, and we out with the bed, and up with a board, and there lay five bouncin' rattlesnakes, and one on 'em had twenty-three rattles on him; and so we killed all on 'em. Now that rattlesnake had *charmed* that child, and for days and days that child would cry till you put it down on the floor, and then 'twould crawl under the bed to that place, and then 'twould be still agin'; and it did seem as though it would never forget that spot, nor snake, and it didn't till we got into the new house.

"Well, this winter we went to scorein' and hewin' timber for the new house, and I followed three scores with a broad-axe, and the timber had to be *hewed* tu; and I was *so tired* many a time, that I wished him and his broad-axe 5000 miles beyond time. Well, I was a hewin' one of the plates, and as 'twas very long, I got one on 'em a leetle windin' and master see it, and he comes along and hits me a lick with the sharp edge of a square right atwixt my eyes, and cut a considerable piece of skin so it lopped down on my nose, and on a hewin' I had to go when the blood was a runnin' down my face in streams; and, finally, one of the men took a winter-green leaf, and stuck it on over the wound, and it stopped bleedin' and it healed up in a few days. This warn't *much,* but I tell it to show the natur' of the man; for any body will abuse power, if they have it to do just as they please.

"Young Tom Ludlow, one of the scorers, comes up to me, arter master was gone, and says he, 'Peter, why in the name of God don't you show Morehouse the bottoms of your feet? I'd be hung afore I'd stand it.' 'Well, Tom,' says I, 'I wants to wait till I knows a little more of the world, and then I'll show him the bottoms of my feet *with a greasein'.* Well, Tom laughed a good deal, and says he, 'that's *right* Pete.'

"Tom was a great friend of mine, and he tried to get me to *run off* for a good while, and Hen, his brother, he was a good feller, and he tried tu; and Miss *Sara,* their sister, she was a good soul, and every chance she got, she'd tell me to run; and Mrs. Ludlow always told me I was a fool for stayin' with *sich a brute;* and every time I went there, I used to git a piece of somethin' good to eat that I didn't get at home; and Mr. Humphrey's folks was all the time a tryin' to git me to run off. 'Why,' they say, 'do you stay there to be beat, and whipt, and starved, and banged to death? why don't you run?' The reply I used to make was, wait till I git a leetle older, and I'll clear the coop *for arnest.*

"Squire Whittlesey, that lived off, 'bout six miles, where I used to go on arrants, says to me one day, 'Peter, where did you come from?' So I ups and tells him all 'bout my history. Then says he, 'Peter, can I put any confidence in you?' 'Yis, Sir,' says I; 'you needn't be afeared of me.' 'Well,' says he, 'you're free by law, and I advise you to run; but, wait a while, and don't run till you can make sure work; and now mind you don't go away and tell any body.'

"And, finally, enemost every body says '*run Pete,* why don't you run?' But thinks I to myself, if I run and don't make out, 'twould be better for me not to run at all, and so I'll wait, and when I run I'll run for sartin.

"There wasn't many slaves in that region, but a good many colored folks lived there, and some on 'em was pretty decent folks tu. Well, we used to have some *'musements* as well as many *sad things;* for arter all Mr. L——, a'most any situation will let a body have some good things, for its a pretty hard thing to put out *all a body's* joys in God's world; and then you see a slave enjoys a good many little kinda comforts that free people don't think on; and if a time come when he can git away from his master, and for-git his troubles, why, he's a good deal happier than common folks. Well, we used to have some very bright times. We had a Fox Tail Company out there of forty-seven men, and Hen Ludlow was captain, and old boss was lefttenant, and I was private, and when we catched a fox, then 'twas *hurrah boys.* Sometimes we used to have a good deal of 'musements over there on Oneida Lake, and we used to have fine sport. We used to start on a kind of a *fishin' scrape,* and come out on a kind of a *hunt.*

"Round that lake used to be a master place for deer. Oh! how thick they was! We used to go over and fish in the arternoon and night; and goin' cross the lake we'd use these 'ere trolein' lines; and then we'd fish by pine torches in the night, and they looked fine in the night over the smooth wa-ter, all a glissenin'; and arter we'd done, we'd sleep on a big island in the lake, near the outlet—they called it the "Frenchman's Island" then, and I guess there was nigh upon fifty acres on it. We'd start the dogs airly next mornin' on the north shore, out back of Rotterdam, and they'd run the deer down into the lake, and then we'd have hands placed along the shore with skiffs, to put arter 'em into the water; and we'd have a sight of fun in catchin' em, arter we'd got 'em nicely a swimmin'.

"There was a lawless set of fellows round that 'ere Rotterdam, that's a fact; and when they heard our dogs a comin' to the shore, they'd put out arter 'em, and if they could git our deer first, they wouldn't make any bones on it: but they never got but *one,* for we used to have young fellers in the skiff that understood their business, and they'd lift 'em along some, I reckon.

"But we used to have the finest sport catchin' fish there you ever see—eels, shiners, white fish, pikes, and cat-fish, whappers I tell ye, and salmon, trout, big fellers, and oceans of pumkin-seed, and pickerel, and bass; and, while I think on it, I must tell ye one leetle scrape there that warn't slow.

"We put up a creek—I guess 'twas Chitining, but I ain't sartin'—a spearin' these 'ere black suckers, and of course we had rifle, powder and ball along. Well, we had mazin' luck, and I guess we got three peck basket-fuls; and at last Tom Ludlow says, 'I swear, Pete, don't catch any more.'

"'Twas now 'bout midnight, and we went back to the fire we'd built under a big shelvin' rock, and pitched our camp there for the night; and this was Saturday night, and we begins to cook our fish for supper. Arter supper, while we was a settin' there, some laughin', some tellin' stories, some singin', and some asleep, the gravel begins to fall off the ledge over us, and rattle on the leaves.

"Well, we out and looked up, and see a couple of lights about three inches apart, like green candles, a rollin' round; and Hen Ludlow says, 'That's a painter, by Judas;' and I says, 'If that's a painter, I've got the death weapon here, for if I pinted it at any thing it must come.'

"Bill, a leetle feller about a dozen year old, says he, 'If I'd a known this, I wouldn't a come;' and so he sets up the dreadfullest bawlin' you ever see.

"Hen says, 'Peter, can you kill that painter?' 'Yis,' says I, 'I can; but you must let me rest my piece 'cross your shoulder, so I shan't goggle, for it's kind'a stirred my blood to see that feller's glisseners;' and he did: so I took sight, as near as I could, right atwixt them 'ere two candles, as I calls 'em, and fired, and the candles was dispersed 'mazin quick. Then we harks, and hears a dreadful rustlin' up there on the rock, and bim'bye a most dole-fullest dyin' kind of a groan; but we hears nothin' more, and so we goes under the rock to sleep, glad 'nough to let all kinds of varmints alone, if they'd only keep their proper distance; but mind you, we didn't sleep any that night. Come daylight, we ventured out, and up we goes on to the rock, and there lay a mortal big painter, as stiff as a poker. I'd hit him right atwixt his candles, and doused his glims for him, in a hurry. Hen, says he, 'Now, Pete, you'll have money 'nough to buy gingerbread with for a good while.' You see there was a big bounty on painters. And I says, 'Hen, if my master was as clever to me as your dad is to you, I should have money 'nough al-ways.' Hen says, 'I shall have my part of the bounty money, and More-house ought to let you have your'n.'

"Arter this, he takes his hide off, and stuffs it with leaves and moss; and we gathers up our fish, tackle, and painter, and starts for home, Sunday mornin'.

"Well, when we got home, master and mistress was glad 'nough of the fish, for they had company. Master's rule was to give me half the fish I got, (I'll give the devil his due,) but this time I didn't git any, and I felt rather hard 'bout it, tu. Hen and Tom says, 'Pete, you call up at our house to night, and we'll settle with you for your share of the bounty for the painter.'

"So I goes to master, with my hat under my arm, and asks him, 'If he'd please to let me go up to Mr. Ludlow's?' 'What do you want to go up to Mr. Ludlow's for?' 'To git my bounty money,' says I. 'No, you main't go up to Ludlow's; but you may go and bring up my brown mare, and saddle her; and du you du it quick, tu.'

"Well, I goes and does what he says; and he goes up to Mr. Ludlow's, and *gits my part of the bounty money, and pockets it up; and that's all I got for dousin' his glims!*

"While he was gone, Lecta, my friend, comes, and says, 'Peter, where's father gone?'

"'To git more painter money,' says I, 'that I arns for him nights.'

"'I think dad's got money 'nough,' says she, 'without stealin' your'n, that you arn nights off on that Oneida Lake.'

"I says, with tears in my eyes, 'I know it's hard, Lecta; but as long as master lives, I shan't git anything but a striped back; and what I arns nights, he puts in his own pockets.'

"'I know it's hard, Peter,' says Lecta; 'but there's an eend comin' to all this; and dad won't live *always, perhaps.*' And I'd often heard her say, arter master had been abusin' on me, 'I declare, I shouldn't be a bit astonished at all, to see the devil come, and take dad off, bodily—*so there.*'

"Well, while I stood there a cryin', out comes Julia, and asks me what I was a cryin' at? 'What's the matter?' says she.

"'Matter 'nough,' says I, 'for master takes all I can arn days and nights, tu.'

"'What?' says Julia, 'dad han't gone up to Ludlow's arter your painter money?'

"'Yes he has,' I says.

"'Well,' says she, 'it's no mor'n you can expect from a dumb old hog.'

Now, that speech come from a *darter,* and a pretty smart darter tu, and it was jist coarse 'nough language to use 'bout master, tu; but Miss Julia never was in the habit of makin' coarse speeches. 'But never mind, Peter,' says she, ''twill be time to take wheat down to Albany, pretty soon, and then you'll git pay for your painter.'

"'Yis,' says I, 'and I'll git pay for a good many other things, tu.'

"Now, Mr. L—, I wants to ax you what reason, or right, there is, in the first place, of stealin' a man's body and soul, to make a slave on him? *and then for stealin' his money he gits for killin' painters, nights?* But the slave ain't a *man,* and can't be, a slave is a *thing;* he's jist what the slave laws calls him, a chattel, property, jist like a *horse,* and like a horse *he can't own the very straw he sleeps on.* But, never mind, there's a judgment day a comin' bim'by. 'And when he maketh inquisition for blood, he remembereth them.' You recollect you preached from that text a Sunday or two ago, and said, if my memory sarves me right, that, at the judgment day, God would require of every slaveholder in the universe, the blood of every soul he bought, and sold, and owned, *as property;* for 'twas traffickin' in the image of the great God Almighty. Ah! that's true, and I felt so when you said it."

A. "Why, Peter, it appears that your master was not only *cruel,* but *mean.*"

P. "*Mean?* I guess he was, why, I'll tell you a story, and when I git to the eend on it, you'll see what mean, means:—

"We lived near the Lake, and master had a fine sail boat that cost a good deal of money, and the young folks round there, that felt pretty smart, used to sail out in it now and then, and I was captain. One day there comes four couples, and they wanted to sail out on the Lake with our gals, and so out we went. Susan Tucker, one of the gals, was a high-lived thing, and the calkalation was, to go down about three miles, and the wind was quarterin' on the larboard side. Well, as I sat on the starn of the boat, she comes, and sets down on the gunnel, and I says, 'Susan, that ain't a very fit place for you to set;' for the wind was kind a bafflin'. She replies, 'I guess there ain't any danger,' and she'd no sooner got the words out of her mouth, than there come a sudden flaw in the wind, and that made the main boom jibe, and it struck her overboard, and on we went, for we had a considerable headway,—well, I let up into wind, and hollered out, 'ain't any body a goin' to help?' and there set her *suitor scart to death,* and all the rest on 'em. Well, I off with all my rags but my pantaloons, and I kept them on out of modesty till the last thing, and then I slipped out on 'em, like a black snake out of his skin, and put out. I swam, I guess, ten rods, and come to where the blubbers come up, and lay on my face, and looked down into the water to see when she come up; and pretty soon I see her a comin', and she come up within a foot I guess of the top, some distance from me, and sallied away agin. I keep on the look out, and pretty soon she comes up agin, and as soon as I see, I dove for her, and went down I guess six feet; and my plan was to catch her round the neck, and when I did, she seized her left arm round my right shoulder, and hung tight. I fetched a sudden twist, and brought her across my back, and riz up to the top of the water, and started for the shore, and I had one arm and two legs to work with, and she grew heavier and heavier, and I looked to the shore with watery eyes, I tell you. Finally I got all beat out, and my stomach was filled with water, and I thought I must give up. Well, while I stood there a treadin' water a minute, I thinks I'd better save myself and let her go, and so not both be drowned. I hated to, but I shook her off my back, and she hung tight to my shoulder, and that brought me on my side; and I kept one arm a goin' to keep us up, and cast my eyes ashore, and gin up that we must go down, and jist that minute a young man come swimmin' along, and sings out, 'Pete, where is she?' and I answers, as well as I could, for I was now a sinkin', and she was out of sight of him, and says, 'under me,' and he dove, and catched her under his arm, and with such force, it broke her loose from me, and off he put for the shore; and I gin up that *I* must sink, and so down I begins to go, and I recollect I felt kind a happy that Susan was safe, if *I* was a goin' to die, for I loved her, and jist then another man come along, and hollers out, 'Pete, give me hold of your hand.' I couldn't speak, but I hears him, and I knew 'nough to reach out my hand, and he took hold on it, and by some means, or other, foucht me on to his back out of the water, and finally got me safe ashore: and sure 'nough, there we all was, and the first thing I knew, he run his finger down my throat, and that made me fling up Jonah, and when I had hove up 'bout a gallon of water, I begins to feel like Peter agin, and I sees I was as naked as an eel, and I set still in the sand. Well, I looked out on the Lake, and there was the boat, and this feller, Susan's suitor, was a rale goslin', and so scart, that he couldn't even jump into the water arter his lady love; and there she was a rockin' in the troughs (*i.e.* the boat,) and one of these same young men that came out arter us, swum out for her, and catched hold of her bow chain, and towed her ashore; and I gits my clothes out, for up to this time I felt egregious streaked, all stark naked there, and I on with my clothes, and goes to Susan, and she was a comin' tu, and as soon as she could speak, she says, 'where's Peter?' I says, 'I'm here, Miss Susan;' and she says, 'and so am I, and if it hadn't a been for you, I should have been in the bottom of that Lake." And while we was a talkin' there, who should come up but her father, and he says, 'my dear child how happened all this?'

"'Pa,' says she, 'it all happened through my carelessness; Peter warned me of my danger, but I didn't mind him, and I fell off."

"'Who saved you out of the water?' says Mr. Tucker; 'that poor black boy there, that's whipped and starved and abused so,' says Susan; then she turns round to me, still cryin', and says, 'Peter, have you hurt you much, my dear fellow?"

"'No, not much, I guess, Miss Susan,' says I. Mr. Tucker then says, 'come darter, can you walk as fur as the carriage?'

"'Yes, Sir,' says she, 'and Peter must go along with us, tu—come Peter, come along up to our house.' 'Yes, Peter, come along,' says Mr. Tucker, a cryin'. 'Yes, Sir,' says I, as soon ever as I've locked the boat;' and he says, 'if you'll *run*, I'll wait for you.' Well, I did run, and lock the boat, and put the key in my pocket, and come back to the carriage, and says he, 'Git in, Peter.'

"No, Sir,' says I, 'I'll *walk.*'

"'Oh! Pa,' says Susan, 'have Peter git in, I want him with us;' and, finally, I got in, and then Mr. Tucker drives on up to his house. When we got opposite master's, Mr. Tucker calls out to him, and says, 'I want to take your

boy up to my house a leetle while;' and he hollered out 'what's the matter?'
So Mr. Tucker tells him all 'bout it; and says he,

"'Nigger, where's the boat?'

"'Locked, Sir.'

"'Where's the key?'

"'In my pocket, Sir.'

"'Let's have it!'

"So I handed it out, and when all on us felt so kind'a tender, and his speakin' *so cross*, and not carein' anything for it, oh! it did seem that he was worse than ever.

"'Go,' says he, 'but be back in season.' Oh! how stern! Well, we comes to Mr. Tucker's house, and Mrs. Tucker cried and wrung her hands in agony; and Rebecca, her sister, cried and screamed, and Edwin, her brother, made a dreadful *adoo;* and Susan says, 'why, don't be frightened so, for I ain't hurt any;' and so we sat down and told all about it, and talked a good while, and Susan said, 'but I shall always remember that I owe my life to Peter, and he's my noble friend.' Well, pretty soon supper was ready; we all sot down, I 'mong the rest, although I was a *poor black outcast*—and Susan, she sat down and drinked a cup of tea, and they wanted her to go to bed, but she wouldn't, and she axed me if I wouldn't have *this,* and if I wouldn't have *that;* and, in fact, the whole family seemed to feel grateful, and I think I never enjoyed myself better than I did at that table. I didn't think so much of the *victuals* as I did of the *folks*.

"Well, arter supper Mrs. Tucker says, 'well, Susan, what you goin' to *give Peter?'*

"'Why, Ma, anything that Pa will let me.' 'Pa says anything, my dear, that Peter wants out of the store, you may give him.'

"So Pa hands Susan the key and says, 'go into the store and give him a good handkerchief, and I'll be in by that time.' So we went in, and she gin me the handkercher, and then Mr. Tucker come in, and took down two pieces of handsome English broad-cloths—oh! how they shone! one piece was green, and t'other was blue, and says he, 'Peter, you may have a suit off of either of them pieces you like best, from head to foot.'

"I says, 'I can't pay for 'em, and master would *thrash me,* if he knew I bought 'em.'

"Mr. Tucker says, 'you've paid for 'em already, and as much agin more;' and I recollect he said some Bible varse, 'as ye did it unto one of the least of mine, ye did it unto me.' And so he measured off two and a half yards of blue for a coat, and one and a quarter green for pantaloons, and picks me out a handsome vest pattern, and three and a half yards of fine Holland linen for a shirt, and threw in the trimmin's—and then picks me out a beaver hat, marked $7 50—then a pair of shoes, with buckles, and turns round and says, 'now, Susan, you take these things up to the house;' and then he gin me a new handsome French crown, and filled all my pockets with raisins, and so we went into the house, and Mrs. Tucker measures me; and Mr. Tucker, says he, 'now, Peter, you'd better run home, and say nothin' to master and mistress, but come up here next Sunday morning, airly.'

"And so I puts out for home, and next day Susan sends for 'Lecta and Polly, our gals, and they stayed there three days, and had what I calls an abolition meetin'; and, arter the old folks was gone to bed one night, 'Lecta comes to me and says, 'Peter, you've got a dreadful handsome suit made;' and Polly says, 'yis, that's what we've been up to Mr. Tucker's so long about,—we've got 'em all done, and a fine Holland shirt for you, all ruffled off for you round the bosom and wristbands, and we want to go up to Ingen Fields to meetin', next Sunday, and I'll ask father to let you drive the iron grays for us.

"Well, Sunday comes, and I goes and tackles up the grays and carriage, and 'twas a genteel establishment, and drove up to the door, and 'Lecta tells me to drive up to Mr. Tucker's, and change my clothes, and leave my old ones up there; and so I drove up to Mr. Tucker's in a hurry, and went in, and Mrs. Tucker, says she, 'now Peter, wash your hands and feet, and face clean;' and I did. And Mr. Tucker says, 'now, Peter, comb your hair;' and I did. Well, he gin me a comb, and so I combed it as well as I could, for *'twas all knots;* and then Mrs. Tucker opened the bedroom door, and says she 'Peter, now go in there and dress yourself;' and I did; and out I come, and she made me put on a pair of clock-stockin's, and she put a white cravat round my neck; and Mr. Tucker says, 'now, Peter, stand afore the glass;' and I did; and then I got my beaver on, and there I stood afore the glass, and strutted like a crow in a gutter, and turned one way and then t'other, and twisted one way and then t'other, and I tell you I felt fine; and Susan says, 'Pa, there's one thing we've forgot.' So she runs into the store and bring out a pair of black silk gloves, and hands 'em to me, and says, 'be careful on 'em, won't you, Peter.' Then I was fixed out, and 'twas the finest suit I ever had. It cost above seventy dollars.

"Well, I took the gals in; and drove over, and took our gals in, and off we started for Ingen Fields. The old folks had gone on afore us in the gig, and we come up and passed 'em, and *if master didn't stare at me, I'll give up.*

"Arter we got there, I hitches my horses, and starts, and walks along to the 'black pew,' as straight as a candle; and I out with my white hand-kercher, and wipes the seat off, and down I sot; and I tell you, *there warn't any crook in my back that day.*

"And master set, and viewed me from head to foot, all day; and I don't b'lieve he heard one single bit of the sarmint all day—he seemed to be thunderstruck. Well, arter meetin' we drove home, and I shifts my clothes, and puts the team out, and comes into the house; and master gives me a dreadful cross look, and says, 'Nigger, where did you git them clothes?'

"'Mr. Tucker gin 'em to me, Sir,' I says.

"'What did Mr. Tucker give 'em to you for?' he says, in rage.

"'For savin' Susan's life, Sir,' I answers.

"'*Susan's life?* you *devil!* What right has Mr. Tucker got to give *you such* a suit of clothes, without my liberty? Hand me that coat.' And I did, but I felt bad.

"Well, he took it, and held it out, and says he, 'Why, nigger, that's a bet-ter coat than I ever had on my back, *you cuss—you;'* and at that he took it, and flung it on the floor in rage. I picks it up, and hands it to 'Lecta, and she puts it in her chist. I had the pleasure of wearing that coat one Sunday more, and then he took it, and wore it out himself!

"The gals says, 'Why, father, *how can* you take away that coat?'

"'Shet *your* heads, or you'll git a tunin'.'

"'Well, father, but how *'twill look*—and what will *Mr. Tucker's folks think of you?'*

"'Shet your dam heads, or I'll take away the rest of his clothes; for he's a struttin' about here as big as a meetin' house. I'll do as I please with my *nig-ger's things!* He's my property!! It's a dam pity if *my nigger's things* don't be-long to me!'[i]

"Now, Mr. L—, he robbed me of *myself,* then of my *money,* and then of my *clothes,* that a good man gin me for savin' his darter's life. Now you see what *mean, means.*

"One day, arter this, I met Mr. Tucker in the road, and says he, 'Well, Peter, how do you git along?' 'Oh! Sir, well 'nough; only master has took my clothes away you gin me, and is a wearin' them out himself.'

"'What!' says he, 'not them clothes I gin you?'

"'Oh! yis, Sir; and I thinks it's cruel to me, and insultin' you most dis-tressedly.'

"'Well,' said Mr. Tucker, 'he ought to be hung up by the tongue atwixt the heavens and 'arth, till he is *dead,* DEAD, DEAD, without any mercy from the Lord or the devil.'"

A. "Well, Peter, I've seen cruel and *mean* things, but that is without exception the meanest thing I ever heard of in my life. Where do you suppose the wretch has gone to, Peter?"

P. "He has gone unto the presence of a God, who hates oppression and oppressors with all his heart; and *God will take care of him,* I tell you, and *he'll do it right tu.*"

A. "Yes, Peter, such men are rebels against Jehovah's government, and it's absolutely necessary for God to punish them, unless they reform; it's as necessary for God to send such men to hell in the world to come, as it is for us to hang a murderer, or put him in prison. And, Peter, which had you rather be, the slaveholder or the slave?"

P. "Domine, I'd rather be the *most miserablest slave in the univarse,* here and herearter, than to be the *best slaveholder* in creation; for I wouldn't, under any circumstances, *own a human bein'.* The sin lies more in the ownin' property in a human bein', than in the 'busin' on 'em, 'cordin' to my way of thinkin'."

A. "You're *right,* Peter; and there will be no progress made in the destruction of slavery, until you destroy the right of property in man!!

ENDNOTE FOR CHAPTER III

i. And with the same propriety, might he say, that his nigger's *soul* belonged to him; or, if he possessed salvation by Christ, that his title to heaven belonged to him. With such premises, he could logically prove that he could *kill* his slave, and do no wrong, as he would innocently kill his ox, or other property. Here we see the legitimate and necessary inference of this barbarous, inhuman and wicked position, that it is right, under certain circumstances, to *own property in man.* A man is not *safe,* as long as he acknowledges this right; for if he believes it *ever* can exist, he will *exercise* it as soon as circumstances are favorable, and become one of the most barbarous and abandoned of slaveholders in an hour.

CHAPTER IV.

An affray in digging a cellar—Peter sick of a typhus fever nine months—the kindness of "the gals"—physician's bill—a methodist preacher, and a leg of tainted mutton—"*master shoots arter him*" *with a rifle ! !*—a bear story—where the skin went to—a glance at religious operations in that region—"a camp meeting"—Peter tied up in the woods in the night, and "expects to be eat up by all kinds of wild varmints"—master a drunkard—owns a still—abuses his family—a story of blood, and stripes, and groans, and cries—Peter finds 'Lecta a friend in need—expects to be killed—Abers intercedes for him, and "makes it his business"—Mrs. Abers pours oil into Peter's wounds—Peter goes back, and is better treated a little while—master tries to stab him with a pitchfork, and Peter nearly kills him in self-defence—tries the rifle and swears he will end Peter's existence now—but the ball don't hit—the crisis comes, and that night Peter swears to be free or die in the cause.

Author. "I've come up again, Peter, to go on with our story, and you can drive the peg while I drive the quill."

Peter. "I had as many friends in that region as about any other man, I reckon, and if it hadn't been for *one man,* I should have got along very well; but oh! how cruel master was. As I was a tellin' on you, we went on buildin' the frame house, and in diggin' the cellar. I was a holdin' the scraper and master was drivin', and a root catched the scraper and jerked me over under the horse's heels, and he took the but eend of his whip, and mauled me over the head; and says I, 'master, I hold the scraper as well as I can, and I wish you'd git somebody that's stronger than me, to do it.

"'Come up here,' says he, as he jumps up out of the cellar, with a halter in his hand, 'and I'll give you somebody that's strong 'nough for you.' Well, I got up, and he makes me strip, and hug an apple tree, and then ties me round it, and whips me with his ox-goad, while I was stark naked, *till he'd cut a good many gashes in my flesh, and the blood run down my heels in streams;* and then he unties me, and *kicks me down into the cellar* to hold scraper agin.

"At that, one of his hired men, who was a shovelin', says, 'Morehouse, you are too savage, to use your boy so, I swear!!' Well, one word brought on another, till master orders him off of his premises. 'Out of the cellar,' says he, in a rage, for jist so soon as he reproved him, he biled like a pot, for you know if a body's doin' wrong, it makes 'em mad to be told on it.

Well, out he got, and says he, as he jumps out on the bank, 'now, More-house, if you are *a man,* come out here tu.' But master darn't do that, for he was a small man. 'Then pay me:' and master says, 'I'll be dam'd if I do.' 'Well,' says the man, 'I'll put you in a way to pay me afore night.' So it comes night, master rides up and pays him, and tries to *hire him agin;* but says he, 'I wouldn't work for sich a barbarous wretch, if you'd give me fifty dollars a day.'[i]

"By being exposed, and abused, and whipped, and almost starved and frozen to death, through the winter, in the spring I was took down with the typhus fever, and lay on a bed of straw, behind the back kitchen door, six months, almost dead; and the doctor come to see me every day, and fi-nally says he to master, 'if you want that boy to git well, you must give him a decenter place to lay than all that comes tu, for 'taint fit for a sick dog.'

"So the gals moved me up stairs, in their arms, and there I lay. They was kind to me durin' my sickness, but master was very indifferent, and didn't seem to care whether I lived or died. Well, the gals, one pleasant day in the fall, took me in their arms, and carried me down stairs, and put me in a little baby wagon, and drew me 'bout twenty rods and back, and then took me up stairs agin', oh! how tired I was, and they did that every day, till I got so I could walk about, and I shall always remember it in 'em, tu.

"Well, in 'bout two months arter this, I got so I could work a leetle, and one day Doctor Walker comes in with his bill of seventy odd dollars; and master says he, '*I wish the dam nigger had died, and then I shouldn't had this money to pay.*' Master payed him off arter some *jawing;* but oh! how savage master was to me arter this![ii]

"Well, next Sunday a Methodist preacher comes along, and was agoin' to preach at Ingen Fields. And so he and his wife come down to dine with us, and we cooked a leg of mutton we had on hand, for dinner, and got it on the table, and all sets down, and master begins to cut it, and come tu, 'twas distressedly tainted around the bone, and smelled bad.

"Well, master orders it off the table; and I goes and knocks over five chickens, and dresses 'em, and friccazeed them in a hurry, and got 'em on to the table; and I guess we didn't hinder 'em mor'n half an hour.

"Well, nobody could stand the mutton, it stunk so; but master tells the folks to give me nothin' else to eat; and I eat, and eat away upon it, day after day, as long as I could; and then I'd tear off bits, and hide 'em in my bosom, and carry 'em out, and fling 'em away, to git rid on it; and one night, when it stunk so bad it fairly knocked me down, I takes the *whole frame* and leaves for the lot with it, and buries it; and thinks, says I, *now* the old mutton leg won't trouble me any more.—But it happened, that a few days arter this, that we was ploughin' that lot, and he was holdin' the plough; and fust he knows, up comes the mutton leg, and fust he looks at it, and then at me, and takes it up, and scrapes the dirt off on it—and oh! how he biled!—and says he, 'You black devil, what did you hide that mutton for?' And he took the whip out of my hand, and cut me with it a few times; and says I, 'Master, I won't stand this;' and off I run towards the house, and he arter, as fast as we could clip it; and he into the house and gits the rifle, and I see it, and oh! how I cleared the coop into the lots; and as I was a goin' over a knoll, he let strip arter me, and I hears the ball whistle over my head. I tell ye, how it come!—and I scart enemost to death.

"Well, I wanders round a while, my heart a pittepattin' all the time, and finally, comes back to the house. But I see him a comin' with the rifle agin' as I got into the lot, and I fled for shelter into the shell of an old hemlock-tree left standin', (you've seen such arter a lot is burnt,) and he see me, and he let strip agin', and whiz went the ball through the old shell, about a foot over my head, for I'd squat down, and if I hadn't he'd a fixed me out as stiff as a maggot. He comes up, and sings out, 'You dead, nigger?' 'Yis, Sir.'

"'Well, what do ye speak for, then, you black cuss?' Then he catches hold on me, and drags me out, and beats me with a club, till *I was dead for arnest, enemost;* and then, lookin' at the hole in the tree, he turns to me, lyin' on the ground, and says, 'Next time I'll bore a hole through *you,* you black son of a bitch. Now drive that team, and straight, tu, or you'll catch a junk of lead into you."

"Well, I hobbled along, and we ploughed all day; and come night, I boohooed and cried a good deal, and the children gits round me and asks, 'What's the matter, Peter?' I tells 'em, 'Master's been a poundin' on me, and then he shot arter me, and I don't know what he will do next.' Julia speaks, and says, 'I declare it's a wonder the devil don't come and take father off.'

"He orders the family not to give me any supper; but arter he'd gone to bed, the gals comes along, and one on 'em treads on my toe, and gin me the wink, and I know'd what it meant; and so I goes into the wood-house, and finds a good supper laid on a beam, where I'd got many a good bite; and went off to bed with a heavy heart.

"But, as I hate to be a tellin' bloody stories all the time, I'll jist give you a short one 'bout a bear; for I was as mighty a hand for bears as ever ye see.

"One night I went along arter my cows into the woods, a whistlin' and a singin' along, with the rifle on my shoulder, a listenin' for my cow-bell, but couldn't hear nothing on it; and so on I goes a good ways, and hears nothin' yit; and I'd hearn old-fashioned people say, you must clap your ear down on the ground to hear your cow-bell, and I did, and I hears it away towards the house; and so for home I starts; and it gits to be kind'a dusk-ish; and the first thing I hears or sees, was right afore me, a great *big black bear,* that riz right up out of the scrub-oaks, and stood on his hind feet; and I was so scart, I didn't know how to manage the business; and there I stood atwixt two evils; one way I was 'fraid of the dark, and t'other I was 'fraid of the bear; and finally, I starts and runs from him, and he jist then down on his legs and put arter me. Well, I turns round and faces him, and he riz up on his hind feet agin', and kind'a growled. Atwixt me and him, there was a small black oak staddle, and thinks I to myself, if I can git to that, I can hold my gun steady 'nough to shoot him; but then I was afeard I shouldn't *kill him;* and if I didn't he'd *kill me.* However, I starts for the staddle; and he kind'a growled, and wiggled his short tail, and seemed to be tickled to think I was a comin' towards him. As quick as I got up to the staddle, I cocked my piece, and aimed right at his brisket, atwixt his fore legs, as near as I could, and fired—*and run;* and never looked behind me, to see whether I'd killed my adversary or not, and put for the house as fast I could. Well, up I come to the house so short-winded, that I puffed and blowed like a steam-boat; and old master says he, 'What you shot, nigger?'

"'A bear, Sir.'

"'Where is he?'

"'In the scrub-oaks, out there; and I b'lieve I *killed* him, tu.'

"'Killed him? you black puppy; go and git t'other rifle, and load it.' And I goes. 'Now,' says he, 'start back for your bear; and if you han't shot any, I'll shoot *you.*' And so back I goes; and master follows along behind me, half scared to pieces, for fear my *dead* bear would bite him.

Well, come to the scrub-oaks, there lay my bear a strugglin', with his fore-paws hold on a scrub-oak, a twistin' it round and round, and *then* master steps up, as resolute as an Ingen warrior, to shoot him, and he first made me fire into his head, and then he fired into his heart; and when we'd killed him *dead,* we draws him to the house and skins him; and I think 'twas the fattest bear I ever see in all my life.

Well, that fall master went to Philadelphia, and he takes that skin with five others I'd killed, that he'd already got the premium on, and sold 'em in Philadelphia—and in all, they come to over one hundred dollars, bounty, skins, and all, to say nothin' at all 'bout *meat;* and he never gin me a Bungtown copper out of the whole. *No,* not enough to buy a pinch of snuff, or a chew of tobacco.[iii]

A. "Were there any churches in that region?"

P. "Yis, Sir; there was two of our gals belonged to the Methodist meetin'—Julia and Polly, and I used to have to drive them to meetin' every other Sunday, to a place about four or five miles off, towards Auburn, called Plane Hill. Every season we used to have a Camp meetin', at what's called Scipio Plains, and used to have to go and strike a tent and carry down the family, and wait on 'em till the meetin' was over. Well, the most I can recollect about them meetin's was, they used to make a despod hollerin' and shoutin'. Some would sing 'glory hallelujah, and 'amen,' and some, 'I can see Jesus Christ, I see him a comin', I see him a comin',' and I was jist fool enough to look and see if I could see him, but I never see anything.

"One Camp meetin' we had I went to, and paid strict 'tention, and it seemed to me that a part of the sarmint was aimed at me, *straight,* but I was so ignorant that I didn't take the sense on it. In what they calls their 'prayin' circles,' there was a colored man—quite an old man, but mighty good, for he made a great prayer; and while he prayed, a good many old and young cried, and shed a good many tears. Well, seein' them cry, made me cry, I 'spose, for I can't assign any other reason; and this colored man see me cryin' and he comes to me and says he, 'my son, do you want religion?' 'Yis, Sir,' says I, 'what is religion?' He speaks in a kind of broken language, and says, 'Religion is to do as we do—sing and shout and pray, and call on God; and don't you want us to pray for you?'

"'Yis, Sir,' says I, 'I wants every body to pray for me.'

"So he speaks to a minister, and says I wants to be prayed for; and so they gits into a ring, and crowds round me like a flock of sheep round a man that's got a salt dish. I don't want to make a *wrong comparison,* but I can't think of nothin' else so near like it. Then this white minister tells me I must git down on my knees; and so down I gits, and they begins to pray, and shout, and sing, and clap their hands, and I was scart, and looked two or three times to git a chance to cut stick and be off, but I couldn't find a place to git out of the ring; and I tell ye, thinks says I, *'if this is religion, I've got 'nough on it, and I'll be off.'* They prayed God would send his *'power,'* and convart that 'ere colored boy; and so while they was shoutin' right down hard for me, one of our gals, Polly, I believe, gits what they calls 'the power,' and they kind'a left me and went over to her; but some on 'em stuck by me, but they didn't seem *nigh so thick,* and I was right glad of that, I tell ye, and as quick as I got a chance, I got out of the ring, and made tracks, and cut like a white head; and when I got a goin' I didn't stop till I got down to the horses, and that was half a mile; and when I got there, the old woman that kept the tavern (she knew me) says, 'why, Peter! what's the matter?'

"'Matter,' says I 'matter enough; they got me into a ring up there, and scart me half to pieces, and I made off, I tell ye; and if scarein' folks makes 'em religious, I'll be a good Christian arter this as any on 'em, for they scart me *like tarnation.*' Well, goin' home that night, the gals talked to me a good deal 'bout religion. They used to be a good deal more religiouser 'bout Camp meetin' times than any other times, and they'd try to git me to pray, and larn me how; and come up into my chamber arter the old folks had gone to bed, to tell me 'bout religion, and all that; and so, arter this meetin' I used to pray some, and when I went arter my cows, I'd git behind some big tree, and pray as well as I knew how, and so every time I got a chance, I'd keep it up, for six or seven months, and then I'd git all over it, and I could swear as bad as ever; and by this time the gals had got kind'a cold, and didn't say much 'bout religion; and that's the history of all my religion then. And arter this *scare* I tell on, I didn't have any more religious fits very soon.

"Prayin' in the woods makes me think of bein' *tied up* there. Once master gits mad with me, cause I didn't plane cherry boards 'nough, and he takes me out into the woods, and ties me up, 'bout dark, and says he, 'now stay there, you black devil, till mornin'.' Well, *he'd whipped me raw afore this,* and there 'twas dark as pitch, and the woods full of all kinds of live varmints,—a sore back, and enemost starved; and I tell ye if I didn't scream jist like a good fellow, I'll give up. I hollered jist as loud as I could bawl, and there I stayed a good while, afeared of bein' eat up by varmints every minute. Finally, a man who hears me, comes up and says, 'whose there?'

"'Peter,' says I.

"'And what's the matter?'

"'Matter 'nough! Master's *whipped me raw,* and enemost starved me, and tied me up, and is a goin' to keep me here all night.'

"'No, he ain't 'nother.' And at that he out with a big jack-knife, and cut the rope; and I says, 'Thank'ee, Sir;' and off he went. But I warn't much better off now, for I darn't go to the house, for there I should git it worse yit; and so I went to the fence, so if any wild thing come arter me, I could be *on the move;* and there I stood, and hollered, and bawled, and screamed, till I thought it must be near mornin'; and finally, one of the gals comes out to untie me; and if ever I was glad to see a women's face, 'twas then; but if there'd been fifty wild beasts within a mile on me, they'd been so scart by my bawlin', that they'd made tracks t'other way.

"But up to 'bout this time, I used to have some sunny days, when I'd enjoy myself pretty well. But I don't think that for five years, my wounds, of his make, fairly healed up, afore he tore 'em open agin' with an ox-goad, or cat-o'-nine-tails, and made 'em bleed agin'. But I've not told you the worst part of the story yit. Master got to be more savage than ever, and so cruel, that it did seem that I couldn't live with him. He got to be a *dreadful drunkard,* and owned a share in a still; and he used to keep a barrel of whiskey in his cellar all the time; and he'd git up airly in the mornin', and take jist enough to make him cross; and then 'twas 'here, nigger,' and 'there, nigger,' and 'every where, nigger,' at once.

"He got to be sheriff, and then he drinked worse than ever; and when he come home, he used to 'buse his wife and family, and beat the fust one he'd come to; and I'd generally be on the move, if my eyes was open, when he got home, for he'd thrash me for nothin'. And I've seen him whip his gals arter they got big enough to be *young women grown,* in his drunken fits; and many a time I've run out, and stayed round the barn, for hours and hours, till I was *nearly froze,* from fear on him; only, sometimes, when I *knew* he *would thrash* somebody, he was *so* savage, *I'd stay in doors, and let his rage bile over on me, rather than on the gals; for I couldn't bear to have them beat so.*

"One day he tells me to git up the team, and go to drawin' wood to the door. I used to have nothin' to eat generally, but buttermilk and samp, except, now and then, a good bite from some of the gals or neighbors. The buttermilk used to be kept in an old-fashioned Dutch barrel-churn, till 'twas sour enough to make a pig squeal. Well, I drawed wood all day, and one of the coldest in winter, and eat nothin' but a basin of buttermilk in the mornin', and so at night I goes to put out the team, and he says, 'Nigger, don't put out that team yit; go and do your chores, and then put up ten bushels of wheat, and go to mill with it, and bring it back to-night *ground,* or *I'll whip your guts out.*'

"Well, I hadn't had any dinner or supper, and it was a tremendous cold night; but 'Lecta puts into the sleigh one of these old-fashioned cloaks, with a hood on it, and says she, 'Don't put it on till you git out of sight of the house, and here's two nut-cakes; and, if I was in your place, I wouldn't let the horses creep, for it's awful cold, and I'm 'fraid you'll freeze.'

"Well, I come to the mill, which was ten miles off, and told the miller my story, and what master said, with tears in my eyes; for my spirit had got so kind'a broken by my hard lot, that I didn't seem to have any thing manly about me. Oh! how you can degrade a man, if you'll only make him a slave!

"The miller says, 'Peter, you shall have your grist as soon as possible,' And I set down by the furnace of coals, he kept by the water-wheel to keep it from freezin', and begun to roast kernels of wheat, for I was dreadful hungry. He axed me to go in and eat; but I didn't want to. And so about twelve o'clock at night I got my grist, and starts for home, and gits there, and takes good care of every thing; and then I begins to think about my own supper. The folks was all abed and asleep; but I finds a basin of buttermilk and samp down in the chimney-corner, and I eats that; and, if any thing, it makes me hungrier than I was afore; and I sets down over the fire, and begins to think!'iv

"I had had many a time of thinkin' afore, but I had never before *felt* master's *cruelty* as I felt it now. Here he was, a rich man; and I had slaved myself to death for him, and been a thousand times more faithful in his business than I have ever been in my own; and yit I must *starve*. I felt the *natur' of injustice most keenly*, and I *bust into tears,* for I felt kind'a broken-hearted and desolate. But I thought *tears wouldn't ever do the work!* I axed myself if I warn't a *man*—a human bein'—one of God's crutters: and I riz up, determind to have justice! 'And now,' says I, 'I may as well die for an old sheep as a lamb; and if there is any thing in this house that can satisfy my starvation, I'll have it, if it costs me my life.'

"So I starts for the cupboard, and finds it locked, and I up with one of my feet and staves one of the panels through in the door, and there was every thing good to eat; and so I eat till I got my *fill* of beef, and port, and cabbage, and turnips and 'taters; and then I laid into the nicknacks, sich as pies, cakes, cheese and sich like. Well, arter I'd one and come out, and set down by the fire, master opens his bedroom door and sings out, 'away with you to bed, you black infernal nigger you, and I'll settle with you in the mornin', and he ripped out some oaths that fairly made my wool rise on eend, and then shets the door. Well, thinks I, if I am to die, and I expected he'd kill me in the mornin', I'll go the length of my rope, and die on a full stomach. So I goes to an old-fashioned tray of nut-cakes, and stuffs my bosom full on 'em, and carries 'em up stairs, and puts 'em in my old straw bed, and I knew nobody ever touched that but Pete Wheeler, and I crawled in and I had a plenty of time to think.

"In the mornin' the old man gits up and makes up a fire, a thing he hadn't done afore in all winter, and them comes to the head of the stairs, and calls for 'his nigger;' and I hears a crackin' in the fire,—and he'd cut a parcel of *withes*—walnut, of course, and run 'em into the ashes, and wythed the eends on 'em under his feet, and takes 'em along,—and a large rope,— and hits me a cut and says, 'out to the barn with me, nigger;' and so I follows him along.

"Well, come to the barn, the first thing he swings the big doors open, and the north wind swept through like a harricane. 'Now,' says he, 'nigger, pull off your coat;' I did.

"'Now pull off your jacket, nigger;' I did.

"'Now off with your shirt, nigger;' I did.

"'Now off with your pantaloons, nigger;' I did.

"'And be dam quick about it too.'

"Arter I gits 'em off, he crosses my hands, and ties 'em together with one eend of a rope, and throws the other eend up overhead, across a beam, and then draws me up by my hands till I clears the floor two feet. He then crosses my feet jist so, and puts the rope through the bull-ring in the floor, and then pulls on the rope till I was drawn *tight*—till my bones fairly snapped, and ties it, and then leaves me in that doleful situation, and goes off to the house, and wanders round 'bout twenty minutes; and there the north wind sweeps through: oh! how it stung; and there I hung and cried, and the tears fell and froze on my breast, and I wished I was *dead*. But back he comes, and says he, as he takes up a *withe*, 'now, you dam nigger, I'm a goin' to settle with you for breaking open the cupboard,' and he hits me four or five cuts with one and it broke; and he catches up another, and he cut all ways, cross and back, and one way and then another, and he whipped me till the blood run down my legs, and froze in long blood isicles on the balls of my heels, as big as your thumb!!!! and I hollered and screamed till I was past hollerin' and twitchin', for when he begun, I hollered and twitched dreadfully; and my hands was swelled till the blood settled under my nails and toes, and one of my feet hain't seen a well day since: and I cried, and the tears froze on my cheeks, and I had got almost blind, and so stiff I couldn't stir, and near dyin'. How long he whipped me I can't tell, for I got so, finally, I couldn't tell when he *was* a whippin' on me!!! 'Oh! Mr. L—,'" said Peter, as the tears rolled down his wrinkled cheeks, while the picture of that scene of blood again came up vividly before his mind, "'oh! Mr. L—, it was a sight to make any body that has got any feelin' weep; and there I hung, and he goes off to the house, and arter a while, I can't tell how long, he comes back with a tin cup full of brine, heat up, and says he, 'now nigger, I'm goin' to put this on to keep you from mortifyin', and when it struck me, it brought me to my feelin', I tell ye; and then, arter a while, he lets me down and unties me, and goes off to the house.

"Well, I couldn't stand up, and there the barn doors was open yit, and I was so stiff and lame, and froze, it seemed to me I couldn't move at all. But I sat down, and begins to rub my hands to get 'em to their feelin', so I could use 'em, and then my legs, and then my other parts, and my back I couldn't move, for 'twas as stiff as a board, and I couldn't turn without turnin' my whole body; and I should think I was in that situation all of an hour, afore I could git my clothes on.

"At last I got my shirt on, and it stuck fast to my back, and then my t'other clothes on, and then I gits up and shuts the barn doors, and waddles off to the house; and he sees me a comin', and hollers out 'nigger, go and do your chores, and off to the woods.'

"Well, I waddled round, and did my chores as well as I could, and then takes my axe and waddles off to the woods, through a deep snow. I gits there, and cuts down a large rock oak tree, and a good while I was 'bout it, tu, and my shirt still stuck fast to my back. I off with one eight foot cut, and then flung my axe down on the ground, and swore I'd *die* afore I cut another chip out of that log that day; and I gets down and clears away the snow on the sunny side of the log, and sets down on the leaves, and a part of the time I sighed, and a part of the time I cried, and a part of the time I swore, and wished myself dead fifty times.

"Well, settin' there I looked up and to my surprise I see a woman comin' towards me; and come to, it turned out to be my old friend 'Lecta, and the first thing she says, when she comes up was, 'ain't you *most dead,* Peter?' 'Yis, and I wish I was *quite,* Miss 'Lecta;' and she cries and I cries, and she sets down on the log and says, 'Peter, ain't you hungry? here's some victuals for you;' and she had some warm coffee in a coffee-pot, and some fried meat, and some bread, and pie, and cheese, and nut-cakes; and says she to me, 'Peter, eat it *all* up if you can.'

A. "Why! Peter what would become of the world, if it warn't for the women?"

P. "Why, Sir, they'd *eat each other up,* and what they didn't *eat,* they'd *kill.* Then they keep the men back from doin' a great many ferocious things. Why, only 'tother day when that duel was fit in Washington, between Graves and Cilley, the papers say that Mrs. Graves, when she found out that the duel was a comin' on, tried to stop her husband, but he wouldn't hear to her, and so he went on, and killed poor Cilley, and made his wife a widder, and his children orphans. Now, only think how much misery would have been spared, if he'd only hear to his wife.

"'Well,' says 'Lecta, 'I wouldn't strike another stroke to day.' And then to be undiscovered, she goes up to a neighbor's and stays there all day. So at night I goes home, and does my chores the best way I could. So I carries in a handful of wood, and master says, 'how much wood you cut, nigger?' 'I don't know, Sir.' 'One load?' 'I don't know, Sir.' 'How many trees you cut down!' 'One, Sir.' 'You cut it up?' 'No, Sir.' 'Well, tell me how much you have cut, dam quick, tu.' 'One log off, Sir.' At that he catches up his cane, and throws on his great coat, and fetches a heavy oath, and starts off for the woods. I sets down in the corner, with a dreadful ticklin' round my heart; and the children kept a lookin' out of the winder, to see him comin', and in he comes, *frothy*, he was so mad. Mistress says to him, 'possup,' which means, 'stop,' I 'spose, and then he went into the other room to supper.

Finally, I crawls into my nest of rags, and I laid on my face all night, I couldn't lay any other way; and next mornin' after tryin' several times, I made out to git up and go down, and do my chores.

"Arter breakfast, Mr. Abers, his brother-in-law, come down, and says he, 'Gideon, what's your notion in torturin' this boy, so? If you want to kill him, why not take an axe and put him out of his misery?' Master says, 'is it any of your business?' 'Yis, Sir, 'tis my business, and the business of every human bein' not to see you torture that boy so. You know he's faithful, and every body knows it, and a smarter boy you can't find any where of his age.[v] Master then colours up, with wrath, and says, 'you or any body else, help yourself! I'll do with my nigger as I please—he's my property, and I have a right to use my own property, as I please. You lie, that it's any of your business to *interfere* with my concerns.'[vi]

"'Don't, you give me the lie again,' says Abers, 'or I'll give you what a liar deserves.' Well, master give him the lie agin, and Abers took him by the nape of the neck and by the britch of his clothes, and flings him down on the floor, as you would a child, (for master was a small man,) and he pounds him and kicks him and bruises him up *most egregiously* and then starts for the door and says, 'come along with me, Peter, you are agoin' to be my boy a spell, and I'll see if this is your fault, or '*master's*' as *you* call him.'

"So I picks up my old hat, there warn't any crown in it, but swindle tow stuffed in, and goes along with him. I gits there, and Mrs. Abers, master's sister, says, 'my dear feller, ain't you almost dead?'

"So arter breakfast, for Mr. Abers had come down afore breakfast, and I sets down and eats with 'em, Mrs. Abers takes a leetle skillet, and warms some water, and then she tries to pull my shirt off, and it stuck fast to my back, and so she puts in some castile soap-suds all over my back, and I finally gits it off, and all the wool that had come off of my old homespun shirt of wool, and the hairs of this, sticks in the wounds, and so she takes and picks 'em all out, and washes me with a sponge very carefully, but oh! how it hurt.—Arter this she takes a piece of fine cambric linen, and wets it in sweet ile, and lays it all over my back, and I felt like a new crutter; and then I went to bed and slept a good while, and only got up at sundown to eat, and then to bed agin. So next mornin' she put on another jist like it, and I stayed there a fortnight and had my ease, and lived on the fat of the land tu, I tell ye."

A. "Didn't your master come after you, Peter?"

P. "Oh! no, Sir; he had all he could do to take care of the bruises Abers gin him. So one Monday mornin' he tells me I had better go home to master's. Well, I begins to cry, and says, 'I'll go, but master will whip me to death, next time.' 'No he won't,' says Abers. 'You go and do your chores, and be a good boy; and I'll be over bim'bye, and see how you git along.'

"Well, as soon as I got home, I opened the door, and mistress says, 'You come home agin', have you, you black son of a bitch?'

"'Yes, ma'am; and how does master do?'

"'None of your business, you black skunk, you.'

"So master finds I'd got home, and he sends one of the children out arter me; and in I goes, and finds him on his bed yit. He speaks, 'You got home, have you?' 'Yis, Sir; and how does master do?' 'Oh! I'm *almost dead*, Peter;' and he spoke as mild as *you* do. And I says, 'I'm dreadful sorry for you;' and I *lied, tu*. So I pitied him, and pretended to feel bad, and cry. And he says, 'You must be a good boy, and take good care of the stock, till I gets well." And so out I goes to the barn, and sung, and danced, and felt as tickled as a boy with a new whistle, to think master had got a good bruisin' as well as myself, and I'd got on my taps first.

"Well, for six months he was a kind of a decent man; he'd speak kind'a pleasant—for he was so 'fraid of Abers, that he darn't do any other way.

"Next winter followin', I was in the barn thrashin'; and, as I stood with my back to the south door, a litter of leetle white pigs comes along, and goes to eatin' the karnels of wheat that fell over master's barn door sill; and I was kind'a pleased to see sich leetle fellers, they always seemed so kind'a *funny;* and the first thing I knew, he struck me over the head with

one of these 'ere old-fashioned pitch-forks, and I fell into the straw jist like
a pluck in a pail of water. I gathers as quick as I could, arter I found out
I was down, and he stood, with a fork in his hand, and swore if I stirred,
he'd knock me down, and pin me to the floor.

"I run out of the big door, and he arter me, with the fork in his hand;
and he run me into the snow, where 'twas deep, and got me to the fence,
where I was up to my middle in snow, and couldn't move; and he was a
goin' to thrust arter me, and I hollers, and says, 'Master, *don't* stick that into
me.' 'I *will*, you black devil.' I see there was no hope for me; and I reaches
out, and got hold of a stake, and as I took hold on it, as 'twas so ordered,
it come out; and, as he made a plunge arter *me,* I struck arter him with this
stake, and hit him right across the *small of his back;* and the way I did it
warn't slow; and he fell into the snow like a dead man; and he lay there, and
didn't stir, only one of his feet *quivered;* and I began to grow scart, for fear
he was dyin'; and I was tempted to run into the barn, and dash my head
agin' a post, and dash my brains out; and the longer I stood there, the worse
I felt, for I knew for murder a body must be hung.

"But bim'bye he begun to gasp, and gasp, and catch his breath; and he
did that three or four times; and then the blood poured out of his mouth;
and he says, as soon as he could speak, 'Help me, Peter.' And I says, 'I
shan't.' And he says agin', in a low voice, 'Oh! help me!' I says, 'I'll see the
devil have you, afore I'll help you, you old heathen, you.' And at that he
draws a dreadful oath, that fairly made the snow melt; and says agin', 'Do
help me, you infernal cuss.' I uses the same words agin'; and he tells me, 'if
you don't, I'll kill you as sure as ever I get into the house.'

"Soon he stood clear up, and walked along by the fence, and drew himself by the rails to the house; and I went to thrashin' agin.' Pretty soon
'Lecta comes out to the barn, and says, 'Peter, father wants to see you.' I
says, 'If he wants to see me mor'n I want to see him, he must come where
I be;' and I had a dreadful oath with it. And she speaks as mild as a blue-
bird, and says, 'Now, Peter, 'tend to me. You know I'm always good to you;
now if you don't mind, you'll lose a friend.' That touches my feelin's, and
I starts for the house; but I 'spected to be *killed* as sure as I stepped across
the *sill.*

"Well, I entered the old cellar-kitchen; and mistress locks the door,
and puts the key in her side-pocket; and master set in one chair, and his
arm a restin' on another, as I set now, and he raises up, and takes down the
rifle that hung in the hooks over his head on a beam; and *I knew I was a
dead man,* for I had loaded it a few days afore for a bear; and says he, as he

fetches it up to his face, and cocks it, and pints it right at my heart. 'Now, you dam nigger, I'll eend your existence.'

"Now death stared me right in the face, and I knew I had nothin' to lose; and the minute he aimed at me, I jumped at him like a *streak,* and run my head right atwixt his legs, and catched him, and flung him right over my head a tumblin', and I did it as quick as lightnin'; and, as he fell, *the rifle went off,* and bored two doors, and lodged in the wall of the bed-room; and I flew and *on* to him, and clinched hold on his souse, and planted my knees in his belly, and jammed his old head up and down on the floor, and the way I did it warn't to be beat.

"Well, by this time, old mistress come, and hit me a slap on the back-sides, with one of these 'ere old-fashioned Dutch fire-slices, and it didn't set very asy 'nother; but I still hung on to one ear, and fetched her a *side-winder* right across the bridge of her old nose, and she fell backwards, and out come the key of the door out of her pocket; and 'Lecta got the key, and run and opened the door—for the noise had brought the gals down like fury; and I gin his old head one more mortal jam with both hands, and pummelled his old belly once more hard, and leaped out of the door, and put out for the barn.

"At night I come back, and there was somethin' better for my supper than I had had since I lived there. I set down to eat; and he come out into the kitchen with his cane, and cussed, and swore, and ripped, and tore; and I says, 'Master, you may cuss and swear as much as you please; but on the peril of *your life,* don't you lay a finger on me;' and there was a big old-fashioned butcher-knife lay on the table, and I says to him, 'Just as sure as you do, I'll run that butcher-knife through you, and clinch it.' I had the worst oath I ever took in all my life, and spoke so savage, that I fairly *scart him.*

"I told him to give me a paper to look for a new master; for you see, there was a law, that if a slave, in them days, wanted to change masters, on account of cruelty, that his old master must give him a paper, and he could git a new one, if he could find a man that would buy him. At fust he said he would give me a paper in the mornin', but right off he says, 'No, I swear I won't; *I'll have the pleasure of killin' on you myself!'*

"So he cussed, and finally, went into the other room; and the gals says, 'Peter, now is your time; stick to him, and you'll either make it better or worse for you.'

"So I goes off to bed, and takes with me a walnut flail swingle; and I crawled into my nest of rags, and lay on my elbow all night; and if a rat or a mouse stirred, I trembled, for I expected every minute he'd be a comin' up with a rifle to shoot me; and I didn't sleep a wink all that night. And I swore to Almighty God, that the fust time I got a chance I'd clear from his reach; and I prayed to the God of freedom to help me get free."

A. "Well, Peter, it's late now, and we'll leave that part of the story for another chapter."[vii]

ENDNOTES FOR CHAPTER IV

i. There are certain *principles,* developed in these facts, which the reader ought to notice. Abolitionists meet with opposition from the slaveholder, and his abettors, for the same reason that this man was cursed by the tyrant who had just lashed Peter! He was angry with the man, *because he told him the truth.* It excited all the malignity of a demon in his breast to be rebuked. He knew he was doing *wrong,* and *conscience* made the reproof a barbed arrow to his soul, and he raved *because his pride was mortified,* and he felt disturbed.—So is it now! The Abolitionists are opposed for the same reason.—They are the first body of men in America, who have depicted slavery—they have dissected the fiendish monster, and brought down the contempt of the world, who love freedom, upon the head of the southern slaveholder. They have poured light, like a stream of fire, upon the whole south, and disturbed the consciences of the buyers and sellers of souls. And we see the malignity of hell itself boiling out of the southern mouth, and southern press; and politicians and religious (?) editors, and ministers of the gospel, are all *pressed* into the vile and low-lived business of bolstering up tyrants upon their unholy thrones, and propping up the darkest, and blackest system of oppression that ever existed on earth. These men have not been needed *before,* their help was not called for;—for nothing was being done to break down slavery. The Colonization Society, met with a different fate at the South, and for this reason it was sustained by all slaveholders who knew the policy. It was the best friend the slaveholder ever had—it kept the consciences of the tyrants quiet—it was a healing plaster just large enough for the sore.—And some of the most distinguished slaveholders in the United States, some of them officers of the American Colonization Society, and the most liberal donors of its funds, told the author of this note, that, *they considered the Society the firmest support slavery had in the world,* for 'twould keep the North and the South quiet about *their peculiar institutions.* "The Society," said one of them, who was at the time a member of the United States Senate, "*has carried away about three thousand or four thousand niggers in twenty years, and the increase has been over half a million. Now, Sir, I can afford, on selfish principles, to give ten thousand dollars a year to that Society, rather than have it go down; for when it goes down, slavery will go with it, and it will go down just as soon as it loses the confidence of the people of the North!!!!!!!* Very good reason why slaveholders should support Colonization!!!!!! There is not the faintest doubt in creation, that the great mass of the South wish slavery, under the circumstances, to continue; and they make war against the Abolitionists because they want it to stop, and are doing all they can to put it down; (for this is the definition of an Abolitionist;) just as the drunkard makes war upon the Temperance Reformation, because it strikes a blow at his idol; just as infidels oppose revivals, because they disturb their consciences, and make infidelity contemptible. Now, I hesitate not to say, that no system of principles, or measures, will ever do away with slavery, except that system which meets with the determined, and combined opposition of slaveholders, and those who are interested in sustaining the system. For the system that destroys slavery, must aim a deadly blow at selfishness, and this will excite malignity, and this will show itself out in the gall that is poured upon Abolitionists, from the cowardly and sophistical apologies of Pro-Slavery Princeton Divines, down to the hard, but not convincing arguments of brick-bats.

The truth is, that the South oppose Abolition, not because "it has put back emancipation," as the New York Observer says,—for, in that case, its champions would be found south of "Mason's and Dixon's line,"—but, because Abolition has a direct, and decided, and tremendous influence in hurling the system of heathenish, and cruel oppression to the ground. *But there are some, a noble, an immortal few, hearts in the South* who are waiting for the consolation of Africa, who bless God for every prayer we offer, and for every convert we gain. And the prayers of every man, and woman, in the slaveholding states, who longs for the freedom of the slave, follow the Abolitionists, and contribute to the spread and triumph of our principles.

ii. One would think that so long a time for reflection, would have softened the poor tyrant's heart—but it is no easy matter to eradicate the tyranny which is fostered in the bosom of the possessor of irresponsible power.

iii. Another exemplification of the abominable doctrine of the right of property in man! Concede this right, and his master did right, and Peter ought not to complain.

iv. *Thought* must ultimately prove the destruction of all oppression. Man is a being of intellect; and if his mind is not so benighted by darkness, or benumbed by oppression, light will find its way into his soul; and his natural love of freedom, and his consciousness of his inalienable rights, will show him the claims of justice, and the deep and awful guilt of slavery; and then he will win his way to liberty, either by *flight* or *blood.* Humanity may be so *chafed* by repeated acts of cruelty and abuse, that any means will *seem justifiable,* in the sight of the being who is to use *some* means for his release, if he ever ceases to groan. It is wisdom, then, to make the slave free while we *can;* for, as sure as God made man for freedom, so sure he will ultimately be free, in one way or another.

v. Here is Abolition, and its opposition in a nutshell. Abolitionists, are those who claim that if a fellow-man is suffering, it is the *business* of his brother to help him, if possible, and in the best way he can. Accordingly, we lift up our voice against the abominations that are done in this land of *chains, and whips, and heathenism, and slaves!* Who are our opposers, and revilers, and enemies? They are men who *don't believe it to be their business,* to interfere with the rights of the slave breeder, and slave buyer, and slaveholder, of the United States. Their creed will let them stand by and look at a brother bleeding, and groaning, and dying under a worse than high-way robbery, and yet 'twill bind their arms if they would extend a helping hand—'twill stop their mouths if they wish to plead for the dumb. Oh! my soul! who that respects the claims of humanity, ain't ashamed to disgrace man so? What philanthropist who wants to see all men rise high in virtue, and happiness, ain't ashamed to hold one set of principles for *men* in *freedom,* and another for *men in chains.* What christian don't blush, to urge as an excuse for chilling and freezing his sympathies for the slave, "the legislation of the country forbids me to help a brother in distress."

vi. The old corner stone of the whole edifice—*property in man.* This reply of the master, is just like the low, and vile swaggering and braging of the South, that has so long intimidated the time-serving *politician of the North, with Southern principles,* and the dough-faced christian with infidel principles. There is something humiliating in the thought, that the South has been able always to put down the rising spirit of freedom at the North, by brags and swagger! Ever since the early days of the Revolution, when Adams and Hancock, and Ames, and Franklin, tried to get the South to wash her hands from the blood of oppression, and be clean, bluster, and noise, and brags have crushed our efforts. And these same patriots, noble in every thing else, were dragooned into submission, and this Moloch of the South was worshipped by the signers of the greatest instrument the world ever saw. And, as the compromise *must go on,* an unholy alliance was formed between liberty and despotism; and as the price paid for the temple's going up, tyranny has made a great niche in our temple of freedom, and there this strange god is worshipped by freemen. Oh! God! what blasphemy is here? tyranny and liberty worshipped together! offerings made to the God of heaven, and the demon of oppression on the same altar!

Nullification lifted its brags and boasts, and swagger, and the North gave up her principles. And because the South has always succeeded, they already boast of victory over all the Abolitionists of the North, and expect either that they have accomplished the work of crushing them, or that they can do it just when they please. But the South will find that since the days of Jay, and Adams, liberty has *grown strong,* and when the great struggle comes, they will see that there are but two parties on the field,—a few slave-driving, slave-breeding tyrants covered with blood, unrighteously shed, at war with the combined powers of the world. The principles of Abolition, have ennobled the human mind, and in all the world's history, cannot be found a body of men, who have endured so much obloquy and abuse, with so much unflinching firmness, and manly fortitude, as the Abolitionists. They are not to be awed by swagger, nor stopped by brags. No! thanks to our Leader, the Lord Jesus Christ, who died to break every chain in creation, the work of human freedom must go forward; and the South has no more power to stop the progress of light, and principles of liberty in this age, than the progress of the sun in the heavens. The great guiding principle of all the benevolence in the world is, to interfere to save a brother from distress and tyranny.—Every reform must interfere with tyranny: 'twas so with christianity in its establishment—with the Reformation—with our Revolution—and shall be so—for christianity makes it man's business to interfere with every usurpation, and system of tyranny and invasion of human rights, until every yoke shall be broken in the entire dominions of God.

vii. All this is a true picture of slavery and oppression, all over the globe. Man is not fit to possess *irresponsible power*—God never designed it; and every experiment on earth has proved the awful consequence of perverting God's design. I know it will be said by almost every reader, who closes this chapter, that this was an isolated and peculiar case; but I know, from observation, that there is nothing at all peculiar in it to the system of slavery; and when the judgment day shall come, and the history of every slaveholder is opened, in letters of fire, upon the gaze of the whole universe, that there will be something peculiarly dark and awful in every chapter of oppression which the universe shall see unfolded. And if I could quote but one text of God's Bible, in the ear of every slaveholder in creation, it would be that astounding assertion—"When he maketh inquisition for blood he remembereth them."

CHAPTER V.

Peter's master prosecuted for abusing him, and fined $500, and put under a bond of $2000 for good behavior—Peter for a long time has a plan for running away, and the girls help him in it—"the big eclipse of 1806"—Peter starts at night to run away, and the girls carry him ten miles on his road—the parting scene—travels all night, and next day sleeps in a hollow log in the woods—accosted by a man on the Skeneateles bridge—sleeps in a barn—is discovered—two painters on the road—discovered and pursued—frightened by a little girl—encounter with "two black gentlemen with a white ring around their necks"—"Ingens" chase him—"Utica quite a thrifty little place"—hires out nine days—Little Falls—hires out on a boat to go to "Snackady"—makes three trips—is discovered by Morehouse—the women help him to escape to Albany—hires out on Truesdell's sloop—meets master in the street—goes to New York—a reward of $100 offered for him—Capt. comes to take him back to his master, for "one hundred dollars don't grow on every bush"—"feels distressedly"—but Capt. Truesdell promises to protect him, "as long as grass grows and water runs"—he follows the river.

Author. "Good evening, Peter,—how do you do to night?"
Peter. "Very well; and how's the Domine?"
A. "Pretty well. Take a chair and go ahead with your story."
P. "My mind had been made up for years to git out of my trouble,—but I thought I'd wait till spring afore I started. Things had got to sich a state, I see I must either stay and be killed myself, or kill master, or run away; and I thought 'twould be the best course to run away; and I wanted good travellin', and I concluded I'd wait till the movin' was good. In the meantime, Master prosecuted Abers for assaulting him in his own house, and Abers paid the damages; I don't know how much; and then Abers prosecuted master afore the same court, for abusin' me, on behalf of the state. His whole family was brought forward and sworn, and testified agin' him, and the trial lasted two days. I was brought forward, and had my shirt took off, to show the scars in my meat; and the judge says, 'Peter, how long did he whip you in the barn?' And I up and told him the story as straight as I could. Then the lawyers made their pleas on both sides, and the case was submitted to the jury, and out they went, and stayed half an hour, and brought in a verdict of abuse, even unto *murder intent.* The judge says, 'how

so?' The foreman on the jury says, 'because he thrice attempted to kill him with a rifle.'

"Well, his sentence finally was, to pay five hundred dollars damages, or to go to jail till he did; and be put under bonds of two thousand dollars for good behavior in future. The judge gin him half an hour to decide in; and he sot and sot till his time was up; and then the judge told the sheriff to take him to jail, and he went to get the hand-cuffs, and put 'em on to master's hands; and the judge says, '*screw 'em tight;*' for you see 'master hadn't treated the court with proper respect,' the judge said. I should think he had the cuffs on ten minutes, and then he says, 'I'll pay the money;' and the sheriff off with the cuffs, and master out with his pocket-book, and counted out the money to the sheriff, and then he gin bail, and so the matter ended.

"The judge come to me and says, 'now, Peter, do you be faithful, and if you are abused come to me, and I'll take care of it.

"Well, all went home, and arter that master behaved himself pretty decent towards me, only the gals said he used to say, 'I wish I'd *killed* the dam nigger, and then I shouldn't have this five hundred dollars to pay.'

"My whole fare was not better, but I still considered myself a slave, and that galled my feelin's, and I determined I'd be free, or die in the cause; for you see, by this time, I'd larned more of the *rights of human natur'*, and I felt that I was a man!!

"I had this in contemplation all of three or four years afore I run, and I swore a heap 'bout it tu. The gals had made me a new suit, and had it ready for runnin' a year afore. The gals paid for it, and kept it secret; and so a woman can keep a secret, arter all; and I had twenty-one dollars, in specie, that I'd been a gettin' for five years, by little and little, fishin' and chorin', and catchin' muskrats, that I kept from master; and I made 'Lecta my banker; and every copper and sixpence I got I put into her hand, and now I'd got things ready for a start.

"Well, the big eclipse, as they called it, come on the 16th of June, 1806, I believe, and we had curious times, I tell ye. I was in the lot a hoein' corn, and it begun to grow dark, right in the day time, and the birds and whip-poor-wills begun to sing, jist as in the evenin', and the hens run to the roost, and I come to the house; and the folks had smoked-glass lookin' through at the sun, and I axed 'em 'what's the matter?' and they said 'the moon is atwixt us and the sun.'

"Well, thinks says I, 'that's rale curious.' Master looked at it *once,* and then sot down and groaned, and fetched some very heavy sighs, and turned pale, and looked solemn; and there was two or three old Dutch women 'round there that looked distracted; they hollered and screamed and took on terribly, and thought the world was a comin' to an eend. Well, I didn't find out the secret of that eclipse, till a sea captain told me, long arter this. I b'lieve this eclipse happened on Tuesday; and next Sunday night, atwixt twelve and one o'clock, I started, and determined that if ever I went back to Gideon Morehouse's, *I'd go a dead man.*

"We all went to bed as usual, but not to sleep; and so, 'bout twelve 'clock, I went out as still as I could, and tackled up the old horse and wagon, and oh! how I felt. I was kind'a glad and kind'a sorry, and my heart patted agin my ribs hard, and I sweat till my old shirt was as wet as sock. So I hitched the horse away from the house, and went in and told the gals, and I fetched out my knapsack that had my new clothes in it, and all on us went out and got in and started off. Oh! I tell ye, the horse didn't *creep;* and the gals begins to talk to me and say, 'now, Peter, you must be honest and true, and faithful to every body, and that's the way you'll gain friends;' and 'Lecta says, 'if you work for anybody, be careful to please the women folks, and if the women are on your side, you'll git along well enough.'

"Well, we drove ten miles, and come to a gate, and 'twouldn't do for them to go through, and so there we parted; they told me to die afore I got catched,—and if I did, not to *bring 'em out.* I told them I'd die five times over afore I'd fetch 'em out; and so 'Lecta took me by the hand and kissed me on the cheek, and I kissed her on the *hand,* for I thought her *face* warn't no place for me: and then she squeezes my hand, and says, 'God bless you, Peter;' and Polly did the same, and there was some cryin' on both sides. So I helped 'em off, and as we parted, each one gin me a handsome half-dollar, and I kept one on 'em a good many years; and, finally, I gin it to my sweet-heart in Santa Cruz, and I guess she's got it yit.

"I starts on my journey with a heavy heart, sobbin' and cryin', for I begun to cry as soon as I got out of the wagon. I guess I cried all of three hours afore mornin', and I felt so distressedly 'bout leavin' the gals I almost wished myself back; but I'd launched out, and I warn't agoin' back *alive.*

"I travelled till daylight, and then, to be undiscovered, I took to the woods, and stayed there all day, and eat the food I took along in the knapsack; and a dreadful thunder-storm come, and I crawled, feet first, into a fell holler old tree, and pulled in my knapsack for a pillar, and had a good sleep; only a part of the time I cried, and when I come out I was very dry, and I lays down and drinks a bellyful of water out of a place made by a crutter's track, and filled by the rain, and on I went till I come to

Skaneatales Bridge; and 'twas now dark, and when I got into the middle, a man comes up and says 'good evenin', Peter.' Well, I stood and says nothin', only I expected my doom was sealed. He says 'you needn't be scart, Peter,' and come to, it was a black man I'd known, and he takes me into his house in the back room, and gin me a good meal. You see I'd seen him a good many times agoin' by there with a team. Arter supper his wife gin me a pair of stockins' and half a dollar, and he gin me half a loaf of wheat bread, and a hunk of biled bacon, and a silver dollar, and off I started, with a kind of a light heart. I travels all that night till daylight, and grew tired and sleepy; and on the right side of the road I see a barn, and so I goes in and lies down on the hay, and I'd no sooner struck the mow than I fell asleep. When I woke up the sun was up three hours, and some men were goin' into the field with a team, and that 'woke me up. I looks for a chance to clear, and I sees a piece of woods off about half a mile, and I gits off; so the barn hid me from 'em, and I lays my course for these woods, and jist by 'em was a large piece of wheat, and I gits in and was so hid I stays there all day; and a part of the time I cried, and sat down, and stood up, and whistled, and all that, and it come night, I started out, and travelled till about midnight, and had a plenty to eat yit.

"Well, the moon shone bright, and I was travellin' on between two high hills, and the fust thing I hears was the screech of a painter; and if you'd been there, I guess you'd thought the black boy had turned white. Well, on the other hill was an answer to this one; and I travelled on, and every now and then, I heard one holler and t'other answer, but I kept on the move; and when the moon come out from a cloud it struck on the hill, and I see one on 'em, and bim'bye, both on 'em got together, and sich a time I never see atwixt two live things. Their screeches fairly went *through* me. Not long arter I come up to a house, and bein' very dry, I turned into the gate to git a drink of water, and I drawed up some, and a big black dog come plungin' out, and in a minute a light was struck up, and out come a man, and hollered to his dog to '*git out;*' and he says to me, 'Good night, Sir; you travel late.' 'Yis, Sir.' 'What's the reason?' And I had a lie all ready, cut and dried. 'My mother lies at the pint of death in the city of New York, and I'm a hastenin' down to see her, to git there if I can afore she dies.' He rather insisted on my comin' in, but I declined, and bid him a good night, and passed on my way. I left the road for fear this man might think I was *a runaway,* and so pursue me; and on I went to the woods. I hadn't got fur afore I hears a horse's hoofs clatterin' along the road; and thinks, says I, 'I'm ahead of you, now, my sweet feller—*I'm in the bush.*' And so I put on; and by daylight I thought I was fur enough off, and I could travel a heap faster in the road, so I put for the road; and nothin' troubled me till ten o'clock. And as I come along to an old loghouse, a little gal came out, and hollers, 'Run, nigger, run, they're arter ye; you're a *run-away, I know.*' I tell you it struck me with surprise, to think how she knew I was a run-away. I says nothin', but she says the same thing agin'; and on I goes till I come to a turn in the road where I was hid, and I patted the sand nicely for a spell I tell ye. When I got along a while, I run into a bunch of white pines; and as I slipped along, I come across one of these 'ere black gentlemen with a white ring round his neck, and he riz up and seemed determined to have a battle with me. Well, I closed in with him, and *dispersed* him quick, with a club; and in about four rods I met another, and I dispersed him in short order; and got out into the road, and travelled till night; and come to a gate, and axed the man if I might *stay with him.* An Ingen man kept the gate, and a kind of tavern, tu; and he says, 'yis;' and I stayed, and was treated *well,* and not a question axed. Well, I axed him how fur 'twas to a village, and he says, 'six miles to Oneida village,' and says he, 'what be you, an Ingen, or a nigger?' I says, 'I guess I'm a kind of a mix;' and he put his hand on to my head, and says, 'well, I guess you've got some nigger blood in ye, I guess I shan't charge you but half price,' and so off I starts. Well, soon I come to a parcel of blackberry bushes, and out come an Ingen squaw, and says, 'sago;' and I answers, 'sagole,' that's a kind of a 'how de.' And all along in the bushes was young Ingens, as thick as toads arter a shower, and I was so scart to think what I'd meet next, my hair fairly riz on eend; and in a minute, right afore me I see a comin' about twenty big, trim, strappin' Ingens, with their rifles, and tomahawks, and scalpin' knives, and then I wished I was back in master's old kitchen, for I thought they was arter me; and I put out and run, and a tall Ingen arter me to scare me, and I run my prettiest for about fifty rods, and then I stubbled my toe agin a stone, and fell my length, heels over head. But, I up and started agin, and then the Ingen stopped, and oh! sich a yelp as he gin, and all on 'em answered him, and off he went and left me, and that made me feel better than bein' in old master's kitchen.

"I travels on and comes to a tavern, and got some breakfast of fresh salmon, and had a talk with the landlord's darter, and she was half Ingen, for her father had married an Ingen woman; and while I was there, up come four big Ingens arter whiskey, and they had no money, and so they left a bunch of skins in pawn till they come back. So I paid him thirty-seven and a half cents and come on. The next time I stopped at a cake and beer shop, and I told the old woman sich a pitiful story, that she gin me all

I'd bought and a card of gingerbread to boot, and I come on rejoicin'. They was Yankee folks, and, say what you will, the Yankee folks are fine fellers where ever you meet 'em.

"Next place I passed was Utica, which was quite a *thrifty little place;* but I didn't stop there; and on a little I got a ride with a teamster down twenty miles, to a place about six miles west of Little Falls, and there I put up with a man, and he hired me to help him work nine days and a half, and gin me a dollar a day, and paid me the silver, and he owned a black boy by the name of Toney. We called him Tone, and they did abuse him bad enough, poor feller! he was all scars from head to foot, and I slept with him, and he showed me where they'd cut him to pieces with a cat-o'-nine-tails. And it did seem, to look at him, as though he must have been cut up into mince meat, almost!!!!

"Well, I left him, and got down about two miles on my journey, and there lay a Durham boat, aground in the Mohawk River; and a man aboard hollered to me, to come down, and he axed me if I didn't want to *work my passage down to Snackady.* I says, '*yis, if you'll pay me for it!!*' You see I felt very independent jist now, for I begun to feel my oats a leetle; and so he agreed to give me twenty shillin's if I would, and so I agreed tu, and went aboard, and glad enough tu of sich a fat chance of gittin' along.

"We come to 'the Falls,' and they was a great curiosity I tell ye; and we got our boat down 'em, through a canal dug round 'em by five or six locks. Oh! them falls was a fine sight—the water a thunderin' along all foam. Well, we had good times a goin' down, and come to Snackady, the man wanted to hire me to go trips with him up and down from Utica, and offered me ten dollars a trip. So we got a load of dry goods and groceries, and goes back for Utica, and gits there Saturday night. The captain of the boat was John Munson, and I made three trips with him, and calculated to have made the fourth, but somethin' turned up that warn't so agreeable. I stayed there Sunday, and Sunday evenin' about seven o'clock, I goes up on the hill with one of the hands, to see some of our colour, and gits back arter a roustin' time about ten o'clock, and as soon as I enters the house, Mrs. Munson says, 'why lord-a-massa Peter, *your master has been here arter you,* and what shall we do?' And I was so thunderstruck, I didn't know what to say, or do. And says she, 'you must make your escape the best way you can.'

"I goes up stairs and gathers up my clothes, and the women folks comes up tu, and while we was there preparin' my escape, old master and the sheriff comes in below! and he says to Munson, who lay on the bed, 'I'm a goin' to sarch your house for my nigger;' and Munson rises up and says, 'what the devil do you mean? away with you out of my house. I knows nothin' about your nigger, nor am I your nigger's keeper—besides, 'afore you sarch my house, you've got to bring a legal sarch-warrant, and now show it or out of my house, or you'll catch my trotters into your starn, *quick* tu.'

"Well, I darn't listen to hear any thing more, but all a tremblin', says I to the women, 'what in the name of distraction shall I do?'

"Mrs. Munson says, 'I'll go down and swing round the well-sweep, and you jump on, and down head-foremost.' I flings out my bundle, and up comes the well-sweep, and I hopped on, and down I went head foremost, jist like a cat, and put out for the river; and I found Mrs. Munson there with my clothes, for she'd took 'em as soon as she could, and put out with 'em for the river. 'And now Peter,' says she 'do you make the best of your way down to Albany, and travel till you git there, and don't you git catched; and so I off, arter thankin' Mrs. Munson, and I wanted to thank Mr. Munson tu, for his management, but I couldn't spend the time, and I moved some tu; and I got down to Albany by one o'clock at night, and there lay a sloop right agin' the wharf, alongside the old stage tavern; and as I was a wanderin' along by it, there seemed to be a colored man standin' on deck, 'bout fifty years old, and his head was most as white as flax, and says he as he hails me, 'where you travellin' tu, my son?' I says, 'I'm bound for New York,' and I out with my old lie agin 'bout my mother. You see that lie was like some minister's sarmints, that goes round the country and preaches the same old sarmint till it's threadbare—but it sarved my turn. 'Come aboard my son, and take some refreshments;' and so I goes down into the cabin, and I feels kind'a guilty, sorry, and hungry, and my feet was sore, for I'd walked bare-foot from Snackady; and if you did but know it, it was a dreadful sandy road, but I wanted no shoes 'bout me that night. Well, pretty soon my meal was ready, and I had a good cup of coffee, and ham, and eggs, and arter that, says he, 'now lay down in my berth;' and I laid down, and in two minutes I got fast to sleep, and the first I knew old master had me by the nape of the neck, and called for some one to help him, and he had a big chain, and he begins to bind me and I sings out, 'murder,' as loud as I could scream, and the old gentleman comes to the berth, and says, 'what's the matter my son?' and I woke up, and 'twas *a dream,* and I was so weak I couldn't hardly speak, and I was cryin' and my shirt was as wet as a drownded rat; and the old man says, 'why, what's the matter, Peter? you're as white as a sheet.' I says, 'nothin' only a dream;' and says he, 'try to git some sleep my son, nobody shan't hurt you.' And so I catches kind'a cat-naps, and then the old man would chase me, and I run into the woods; and three or four men was arter me on white horses, and I run into a muddy slough, and jumped from bog to bog, and slump into my knees in the mud, and I'd worry and worry to git through, and at last I did; and then I had to cross a river to git out of their way, and I swum across it, and it was a pure crystal stream, and I could see gold stones and little fish on the bottom. Well, I got to the bank and sets down, and they couldn't git to me, and I had a good quiet sleep. Finally, the old man comes to me, and says, 'come, my son, git up and eat some breakfast. And I up, and the sun was an hour high, and more tu. I washes me, and we had some stewed eels and coffee; and we eat alone, for all the hands and captain was a spendin' the night among their friends ashore. And the old man begins to question me out whether I warn't a run-away, and I rother denied it in the first place; and he says, 'you needn't be afeard of me. You're a run-away, and if you'll tell me your story, I'll help you.' So I up and told him my whole story, and he says, 'I know'd you was a run-away when you come aboard last night, for I was once a slave myself, and now arter breakfast you go with me, and I'll show you a good safe place to go and be a cook.'

"So we walked along on the dock, and says he, 'there comes the Samson, Captain John Truesdell, I guess he wants you, for I understood his cook left him in Troy.'

"So the Samson rounded up nigh our'n, and the captain jumps ashore, and says he, 'boy do you want a berth?' and I touches my hat, and says, 'yis, Sir.' And he says, 'can you roast, bake, and bile, &c.?' I says, 'I guess so.' 'Can you reef a line of veal, and cook a tater?' 'Yis, Sir, all that.' 'Well, you are jist the boy I want; 'what do you ask a month?' I says, 'I don't know;' but I'd a gone with him if he hadn't agin me a skinned sixpence a month. Well, he looks at me, and slaps me on the shoulder, and says he, 'you look like a square-built clever feller,—I'll give you eight dollars a month.'

"This colored man looks at me and shakes his head, and holds up all hands, and fingers, and thumbs, and that's ten you know. So I axed him ten dollars a month. And says he, 'I'll give it;' and my heart jumps up into my mouth. And he claps his hand into his pocket, and took out three dollars, and says he, 'now go up to the market and git two quarters veal, and six shillin' loaves of bread, and here's the market basket.' Well, I thought it kind'a strange that he should trust me, cause I was a stranger; but I found out arter this, a followin' the seas, that it was the natur' of sailors to be trusty. Well, I off to the market, and I goes up State-street and looked across on 'tother side, and who should I see but *Master and the Sheriff*, a comin' down; so I pulls my tarpaulin hat over my eyes, for I'd got all rigged out with a sailor suit on the Mohawk, and I spurs up, and the grass didn't grow under my feet any nother. I does my business, and hastens back as fast as possible, and got aboard, and the captain made loose, and bore away into the wind, and made all fast; and the sails filled, and down the river we went like a bird. A stiff breeze aft, and I was on deck, for I wanted to see, and the captain comes along and says, 'boy, you'd better below,' and down I went. Well, we run under that breeze down to the overslaugh, and got aground, and then my joy was turned into sorrow. The captain says to me, 'boy, you keep ship while I and the hands go back and git *a lighter,* or we shan't git off in a week; and he takes all hands into the jolly boat and starts for the city again. Arter they'd gone I wanders up and down in the ship, and cried, and thought this runnin' aground was all done a purpose to catch me; and I goes down into the cabin and ties all my clothes up in a snug bundle, and goes into the aft cabin, and opens the larboard window, and made up my mind that if I see any body come that looked suspicious, I'd take to the water.

Well, afore long, I see the jolly boat a comin' down the river, and every time the oars struck she almost riz out of the water. Three men on a side and the captain sot steerin' and as she draws nigher and nigher I draws myself into a small compass, for I was afeard master was aboard that boat. Well, she comes alongside, but thanks to God no master in that boat.

"The captain comes on deck and says with a smile, '*Peter, you may git din-ner now.*ⁱ So I goes and gits a good dinner, for I understood cookin' pretty well, and they eats, and I tu, and then I clears off the table, and washes the dishes, and sweeps the cabin, and goes on deck. And sees a lighter comin' down the river, and she rounded up and come alongside, and we made fast, and up hatches and took out the wheat, and worked till evenin', and then she swung off; and by mornin' we'd got all the freight aboard, and we discharged the lighter and highted all sail, and the wind was strong aft, and we lowered sail no more till we landed in New York, and that was the next day at evenin'.

"Well, the second night arter this, the captain come down into the cabin, and says he, 'Peter, I've got a story for you. 'Well,' says I, 'I wants to hear it, Sir.' 'Well last night there was a small man from Cayuga county, by the name of Gideon Morehouse come aboard my sloop, and says, "you've got my nigger concealed aboard your ship, and I've got authority to sarch your vessel, 'and he sarched my vessel and every body and every thing in it, and by good luck *you* was ashore, or he'd a had you; for you must be the boy by description.'

"Now I was on the poise whether to tell the truth or not; but I was rather constrained to lie; but the captain says, 'tell me the truth, Peter, for t'will be better for you in the eend; so I up and told him my whole story, as straight as a compass, and long as a string.

"'Well' says he, 'be a good boy, and I'll take care on you.' So we stayed in New York a few days, and back to Albany, and started for New York agin and we had fourteen pretty genteel passengers, and the captain says, 'now Peter be very attentive to 'em and you'll git a good many presents from 'em.' 'So I cleaned their boots and waited on 'em, and when I got to York I carried their baggage round the city, and when I got to the sloop I counted my money, and had six dollars fifty cents, jist for bein' polite, and it's jist as easy to be polite as any way.

"Well, the next mornin' the captain comes to me about daylight, and hollers, 'up nig, there's a present for you on deck.'

"So I hops up in great haste and there was stuck on the sign of the vessel, an advertisement, and 'reward of one hundred dollars, and all charges paid for catchin' a large bull-eyed Negro, &c.' The captain reads that to me, and says very seriously, 'Peter that's a great reward. You run down in the cabin and git your breakfast, I must have that hundred dollars; for one hundred dollars don't grow on every bush.'

"Well, I started and went down, a sobbin' and cryin' to get breakfast, and calls the captain down to eat, and he sets down and says he, 'Peter ain't you agoin' to set down and eat somethin'? it will be the last breakfast you'll eat with us.'

"I says with a very heavy heart, 'no Sir, I wants no breakfast.' Arter breakfast says he, 'now clear off the table, and do up all your things nice and scour your brasses, so that when I get another cook he shan't say you was a dirty feller.' So I goes and obeys all his orders, and I shed some tears tu, I tell ye; and then I set down and had a regular-built cryin' spell, and then the captain comes down and says, 'you done all your work up nicely?' 'Yis Sir,' 'well, now go and tie up all your clothes.' So I did, and I cried louder than ever about it, and he says, 'I guess you han't got 'em all have ye?' So he unties my bundle, and takes all on 'em out one by one, and lays 'em in the berth, and I cried so you could hear me to the forecastle; and finally he turns to me a pleasant look and says, 'Peter put up your clothes; I've no idea of takin' you back, I've done this only to try you; and now I tell you on the *honor of a man,* as long as you stay with me, and be as faithful as you have been, nobody shall take you away from me *alive;* and then I cries ten times worse than ever, I loved the captain so hard. But a mountain rolled off on me, for I tell you to be took right away in the bloom of liberty, arter I'd toiled so hard to git it, and then have all my hopes crushed in a minute, I tell you for awhile I had mor'n I could waller under. But when I got acquainted with the captain, I found him a rale abolitionist, for he'd fight for a black man any time, and Oh! how he did hate slavery: but then he kind'a loved to run on a body, and then make 'em feel good agin, and he was always a cuttin' up some sich caper as this; but he was a noble man and I love him yit.

"Now I felt that I was raly free although I knew Morehouse was a lurkin' round arter me; *and arter this I called no man master,* but I knew how to treat my betters. I now begun to feel somethin' like a man, and the dignity of a *human bein'* begun to creep over me, and I *enjoyed* my liberty when I got it, I can tell you. I didn't go a sneakin' round, and spirit-broken, as I know every man must, if he's a slave; but I couldn't help standin' up straight, arter I knew I was free. Oh! what a glorious feelin' that is! and oh! how I pitied my poor brethren and sisters, that was in chains. I used to set down and think about it, and cry by the hour; and when I git to thinkin' about it now, I wonder how any good folks, and specially christian people, can hate abolitionists. I think it must be owin' to one of two things; either they don't know the horrors or miseries of a slave's life, or they can't have much feelin'; for the anti-slavery society is the only society I know on, that professes to try to set 'em all free; for you know the colonization folks have give up the idee long ago, that they can do any thing of any amount that way; and so they say they are agoin' to enlighten Africa. And I can't for the life on me see how the abolitionists is so persecuted; it's raly wonderful! But I'm glad I can pray to God for the poor and oppressed, if I am a black man; and I think it can't be a long time afore all the slaves go free—there is so many thousands of christians all prayin' for it so arnestly; and so many papers printed for the slave, and so many sarmints preached for him, and sich a great struggle agoin' on for him all over creation. Why all this is God's movin's, and nobody can't stop God's chariot wheels."

A. "Well, Peter, you've come to a stopping place now, and I think we'll close this book, for I suppose you'll have some sea stories to tell."

P. "Yis, Domine. I shall have some long yarns to reel off when I gets my sails spread out on the brine, for I think the rest of my history is no touch to my sailor's life. But one thing, it won't be so sorrowful, if 'tis strange; for, if I was rocked on the wave, I had this sweet thought to cheer me, as I lay down on my hammock, *I'm free;* and dreams of liberty hung round my midnight pillow, and I was happy, because I was no longer Peter Wheeler in chains."

~

Thoughts suggested by the incidents of the First Book.

It may be profitable and interesting to notice some of the principles involved in the foregoing story. The history of Peter Wheeler in Chains, is a rich chapter in the tale of oppression and slavery in America. The horrors and barbarities here recorded, ought not to go forth before the citizens of a free nation, without producing an appropriate and powerful impression, that will give *impulse* and triumph to the principles of our constitution. A few plain thoughts occur to the reader of this history, which we will notice:—

I. We see the necessary and legitimate influence of irresponsible power, upon its possessor and victims. It is one of the broad principles of the bible, and of our republican government, that it is not safe to place irresponsible power in the hands of a fallible being, under any circumstances; for, in every recorded instance of the world's history, it has been abused, and produced unmixed misery.

When young Nero assumed the purple of imperial Rome, his heart revolted at the thought of tyranny, and when first asked to sign a criminal's death-warrant, his hand refused to do its office-work, and he exclaimed, "Would to God I had never learned to write." And yet, under the influence of irresponsible power, he at last became so transformed, that he illuminated his gardens with the bodies of burning Christians, and danced to the music of a drunken fiddler while Rome was on fire! As man is constituted, he is not equal to a possession of unlimited power, without abusing it. Experience confirms all this, and common sense too. And if the history of every slaveholder in creation could be unfolded, we should see that every hour his character acquired new and worse features. Even if he did not gradually become more hard and tyrannical in his treatment of his slaves, yet it would be seen that his own heart was constantly losing its higher and nobler qualities, and the dark trail of oppression, like the course of the serpent, was leaving its foul and polluted stain upon all it touched. Slavery *must* call forth malignant and unholy passions in the breast, and their repeated exercise must harden and pollute the heart. It degrades the *whole man,*—for there is not a faculty or propensity of the being but what is tainted by the foul breath of slavery. The reader must have remarked the steady and rapid moral defilement which was going on in Peter's master, till at last he was plunged into the deepest degradation, which sought *his death.* Oh! who can conceive of a degradation more complete than that which made its subject exult in the thought of torturing a poor black boy, even unto death! There are noble and generous hearts in the South, who feel, most keenly, the debasing influence of slavery upon the father's, and the husband's, and the lover's heart; and they are weeping, in secret places, because every green thing around the social altar is burned up by this withering blast. The author of this note has heard the lamentations of daughters and wives, whose homes have been made desolate by the foul spirit of tyranny, and their longings and prayers for a brighter day, which shall regenerate the South by emancipating the slave. Oh! how can man become viler than to hunt down the poor fugitive slave, like a bloodhound, when he has cast off his fetters, and is emerging into the light and glory of freedom. The first impulse of a generous or benevolent heart would be joy, to see the poor victim break away from his bondage, and to go free, in God's beautiful world. Let us hear no more of the desire of the South to emancipate their slaves, when every fugitive is tracked by bloodhounds, till he crosses the waters of the St. Lawrence, and finds shelter under the throne of a British Queen. In most instances, slavery will make the master thirst for the blood of the slave who escapes from his chains; and let this fact bespeak its influence on his heart.

II. Opposition to anti-slavery principles, is no new thing under the sun. We should conclude, from the reasoning of some, in these days, that all efforts made to suppress slavery, which elicit the opposition of the South, must be wrong, for, say they, "slavery can be destroyed without any opposition from the slaveholder!"

Monstrous!!! what? the most stupendous structure of selfishness and abominations on earth, be uptorn without opposition or convulsion! As well may you say, that God could have emancipated the Hebrews, without exciting so much opposition from their masters! The truth is, that the doctrine was never broached till these latter days, that freedom could be achieved without a struggle. As well say that our fathers could have achieved the independence of '76 without opposition. The experiment was made for twenty years, by colonizationists, to do away with slavery, without opposition, and, accordingly, they were obliged to mould their scheme and plans to suit the South, so as to avoid opposition; and the South succeeded, and gave them a scheme which would transport to a dark, and desolate, and heathen shore, to die of starvation, four or five thousand, while the increase was 700,000, to say nothing of the old stock on hand. Good reason why the South should not oppose such a plan. They would display unutterable folly in their opposition.

Slavery is one of the strongholds of hell, and it is not to be torn down without a struggle, any more than satan will surrender any other part of his kingdom without opposition. Peter's master was enraged at any reproof or interference from others, that came in collision with his tyranny, and so it is now.

III. We see, also, that the slave, in all ages, thinks so badly of slavery, that he is disposed to run away, if he can. This is enough to say about slavery. Men are not disposed to run away from great blessings. And yet we are told, constantly, by the South, that the slaves are contented and happy with their masters. Now, if this is true, it only makes slavery worse; for what kind of a system is that which degrades a man so low, and prostrates all his better and more glorious attributes to such degradation, that *the love of liberty is crushed in his soul;* that no heaven-directed thought is lifted for the high enjoyments of an intellectual and bright being; that he is stripped of all that he received from Jehovah, which elevates him above the worm that crawls at his feet. Oh! fellowman beware! if you have succeeded so completely in defacing the lineaments of divinity in the human soul, that all the glorious objects of creation will not draw forth from his bosom a thought or a wish after a brighter abode. If the gay carol of the wild bird, or the fresh breezes of morning which bring it to his ear, or the stars of heaven, as they roll in their orbits, or the bright dashing of the unfettered waters which sweep by, or the playful gambols of the lamb that skips and plays on their banks; or, above all, if the spirit of the Eternal Father, which breathes nobility and greatness into the soul of his children, does not fan the fires of liberty in his bosom; oh! fellow-man, if you have so completely dashed to oblivion and nothingness, an immortal spirit, you have done a deed at which all hell would blush; you have covered the throne of the Eternal in mourning. If this be true, you are worse than you have ever been described.

But, Sir, your whole enginery of death has never accomplished such a total destruction as this. You may have *degraded mind,* and you *have,* but oh! thanks to God, you have not made such awful havoc with a deathless spirit as this. No! you have only poured gall into wounded spirits; you have only torn open deeply lacerated bosoms;—you have only plucked the most glorious pearl from man's diadem; you have only heaped insult upon a son or a daughter of God Almighty, who is redeemed by the blood of the Lamb;—and your stroke or bolt of wo, that unchained the spirit, only open a passage-way for it to the gates of eternal glory. But, you have done enough God knows! You have done enough to heap up fuel for your own damnation; and encircled by those faggots, "you shall burn, and none shall quench them," through eternal ages, unless you are cleansed by atoning blood.

The truth is yet to be told. The slave is not contented and happy—more, no slave in the universe ever was, or can be contented, till God shall strip him of his divinity which makes him a man. I have conversed with several thousands in bondage, and many who have got free, and never did I hear such a sentiment full from human lips. It is estimated by facts already in our possession, (viz. the numbers who win their way to freedom, and those who are advertised as run-aways who are caught,) that more than fifty thousand slaves attempt their escape from bondage every year. And yet so anxious are their masters to still bind the chains, that many of them are chased over one thousand miles. What bare-faced hypocrisy in a man, to give money to transport to an inhospitable and barbarous clime, a worn-out slave, and yet to chase *his brother* one thousand miles to reduce him again to bondage, or to death!!

IV. *The low and base meanness of slave-holding.* Nothing is accounted *meaner* than theft and *stealing!* And yet every slaveholder is necessarily a constant, and perpetual thief. He steals the slave's body and soul. And if there is one kind of theft which is worse than all others, it is to steal the wages of the poor, three hundred and sixty-five days in the year! It would be accounted very mean in a rich man, to employ a poor day laborer and then follow him to his home at night, after the toils of the day were over, and steal from his pocket the price of his day's labor, which he had paid to him to buy bread for his children, and such a man would be called a wretch all over the world;—and yet every slaveholder as absolutely steals the slave's wages every night—for he goes to his dwelling and family, if he have one, pennyless after a day of hard toil. It would be considered the worst kind of *meanness* to go, and divide, and separate by an impassable distance the members of a poor family; and yet not a slave lives in the South, who has not at some time or other, seen the same barbarous practice in the circle of his own relationship, and love.

It is the necessary and legitimate inference of the master, from the doctrine of *the right of property in man,* that all the slave possesses or acquires belongs to the one who owns him. Accordingly, Morehouse had a *perfect right* to the broadcloth coat which Mr. Tucker gave Peter for saving the life of his daughter. The whole difficulty, the grand cause of all the barbarities of slavery, lies in this unfounded and infamous claim of the right to own, as property, the image of the Great Jehovah. Destroy this claim, and slavery must cease forever. Acknowledge it in *any instance,* or *under any circumstances,* and the flood-gate is flung wide open to the most tyrannical oppression in an hour. This was illustrated in the case of Dr. Ely, of Philadelphia, who pretended to be "opposed to slavery as much as any body," and yet who still maintained *that corner-stone principle of tyranny, "that it is right under certain circumstances to hold man as property."* He removed to a slave state, and found that "these circumstances" occurred. He *bought a slave, Ambrose,* with, (as he declared,) *benevolent designs,* intending to spend the avails of his unrequited labor, in buying others to emancipate. He was expostulated with by his brethren in the ministry, and out of it, against the *sin of his conduct in owning a fellow-man,* and making the innocent labor without reward, to free the enslaved. And "the hire of the laborer which he kept back cried to God." He was told of the *danger of owning a man for an hour,* by a keen-sighted editor of New York; and this same editor uttered a prophecy which seemed almost like the voice of inspiration, that God would pour contempt upon such an unholy experiment, "of doing evil that good might come." But still the Doctor passed on, and heeded it not. At length, after that prophecy had been forgotten by all but the friends of the slave, its fulfilment came from the shores of the Mississippi, and God had blasted the Doctor's unrighteous scheme, and his speculations all failed, and poor Ambrose was sold to pay his master's debts. Then the experiment was fairly, and one would think, *satisfactorily* made, and the principle was settled forever by God's providence, that "*it is wrong under any circumstances to hold man as property.*" We want the slaveholder to give up his unholy, and unfounded claim to the image of God, and when he will practically acknowledge this principle, then he will cease to be a slaveholder.

V. We see, in the light of this story, the debasing, degrading, and withering influence of slavery upon its poor victim. Peter tells the truth, when he says, "no man can hold up his head *like a man* if he is a slave." Any person who has been on a southern plantation must confess, that there is a degraded and servile air upon the countenance of all the slaves. A more abject, low, vacant, inhuman look, cannot be seen in the face of a being in the world, than you see when you meet a southern slave. It is not the tame and subdued look of a jaded beast. It is infinitely more painful to behold a slave than such a spectacle. He seems to be a man with the soul of a beast; God's image does not speak from his dim and lustreless eye, or his lifeless and degraded bearing. You see a human form, but you cannot see the image of his Maker and Father there. The slave loses his self-respect, and all regard for his nature. He is shut out from all the lovely and glorious objects of creation; and a soul which was made to soar upward in an eternal flight towards its Sire, is smothered, and debased, and ruined;—its existence is almost blotted from creation, and when it leaves its abused and lacerated house of mortality, the world does not feel the loss;—the departure is unnoticed, except by a few who loved him in life, and are glad when his pilgrimage is over. The spirit flies, "no marble tells us whither;" and he is forgotten, and only a few like himself know that he ever existed in a green and beautiful world. But "a soul is a deathless thing," and that soul shall *speak* at the last judgment day! It shall tell its tale of blood to an assembled universe, and that universe shall pronounce the doom of its murderer. In forecasting the proceedings of the last day, I tremble to think I shall be one of its spectators; *not because I shall be tried,* for I humbly trust I shall have an advocate there, whose plea the Judge will accept, and whose robe of complete righteousness shall mantle my naked spirit. But the revelations of that solemn tribunal, which millions of enslaved Africans shall unfold, will make the universe turn pale. And I should feel a desire to withdraw behind the throne, till the sentence had been passed upon all buyers, and sellers, and owners, of the image of the Omnipotent Judge, and executed; did I not wish to behold *all the scenes* of that great day, and mingle my sympathies with *all the fortunes of that Throne.* For, as I expect to stand among that mighty company, who shall cluster around the Judgment Seat, *I do believe, that God's Book will contain no page so dark with rebellion and crime, as that which records the story of American Slavery!* And yet I believe that that Book will embrace the history of the whole creation.

VI. We see the glorious and hallowed influence of freedom upon man:—No sooner had Peter escaped from chains, than he began to emerge from degradation into the dignity of a human being. He breathed an inspiring and ennobling atmosphere; he felt the greatness and glory of immortal existence steal over him, and his soul, which had been shrouded in darkness, begun to lift itself up from a moral sepulchre, and feel the life-giving energy of a resurrection from despair. It must have been so, for man's element is freedom, and it cannot live in any other; deprived of its necessary element, it will languish and die.

While I am writing this paragraph, Peter Wheeler comes into my room, and we will hear his own testimony; he says, "Arter I'd got my liberty, I felt as though I was in a *new world;* although I suffered, for a while, a good deal, with fear of being catched.

"When I look back, and think how much I suffered by bein' beat, and banged, and whipt, and starved; and then my feelin's arter I got free, when I held up my head among men, and nobody pinted at me when I went by and said, 'there goes this man's nigger, or that man's nigger;' why, I can't describe how I felt for two or three years. I was almost crazy with joy. What I got for work was *my own,* and if I had a dollar, I would slap my hand on my pocket and say, '*that's my own;*' and if I hauled out my turnip, why it ticked for me and not for master, and 'twas mine tu when it ticked. And I bought clothes, and good ones, and my own *arnin's* paid for 'em. In fact, I breathed, and thought, and acted, all different, and it was almost like what a person feels when he is changed from darkness into light. Besides, when gentlemen and ladies put a handle to my name, and called me *Mr. Wheeler,* why, for months I felt odd enough; for you see a slave han't got no name only 'nig,' or 'cuss,' or 'skunk,' or 'cuffee,' or 'darkey;' and then, besides, I was treated like a man. And if you show any body any kindness, or attention, or good will, you improve their characters, for you make them respect you, and themselves, and the whole human race a sight more than ever. Why, respect and kindness lifts up any body or thing. Even the beast or dog, if you show 'em a kindness, they never will forgit it, and they'll strut and show pride in treatin' on you well; and pity if man is of sich a natur' that he ain't as noble as that, then I give it up. Why, arter I come to myself, and I would git up and find all the family as pleasant as could be, and I would go out and look, and see the sun rise, and hear the birds sing, and I felt so joyful that I fairly thought my heart would leap out of my body, and I would turn on my heel and ask myself 'is this Peter Wheeler, or ain't it? and if 'tis me, why how changed I be.' I felt as a body would arter a long sickness, when they first got able to be out, and felt a light mornin' breeze comin' on 'em, and a fresh, cook kind of a feelin' comin' over 'em; and they would think they never see any thing or felt any thing afore, for all seemed brighter and more gloriouser than ever; and oh! it does seem to me that no Christian people in the world can help wantin' to see all free, for Christians love to see all God's crutters happy.

VII. "I b'lieve that one of the wickedest and most awful things in creation, and the root, and bottom, and heart of all the evil, is prejudice agin' color." There is most, or quite as much of this at the North as there is at the South, for I can speak from experience. There is that disgrace upon us, that many people think it's a disgrace to 'em to have us come into a room where they be, for fear that they will be *blacked*, or *disgraced*, or *stunk* up by us poor off-scourin' of 'arth. And if I come into a room with a sarver of tea, coffee, rum, wine, or sich like, they can't smell any thing; but jist the second I set down on an equal with 'em, as one of the company, they pretend they can smell me. But, worse than this, this same disgrace is cast on our color in the Sanctuary of the Living God. In enemost all the meetin' houses, you see the 'nigger pew;' and when they come to administer the Lord's Supper, they send us off into some dark pew, in one corner, by ourselves, as though they thought we would disgrace 'em, and stink 'em up, or black 'em, or somethin'. Why, 'twas only at the last Sacrament in our Church this took place. All communicants was axed to come and partake together, and I come down from the gallery, and as I come into the door, to go and set down among 'em; one of the elders stretched out his arm, with an air of disdain, and beckoned me away to a corner pew, where there was no soul within two or three pews on me, as though he had power to save or cast off. Now think what a struggle I had, when I sot down, to git my mind into a proper state for the solemn business I was agoin to do.

"First, I thought it was hard for me to be so cast off by my brethren in the church, and a feelin' riz, and I fit agin' it, and, finally, I thought I could submit to my fate; and I believed God could see me, and hear my cry, and accept my love, as well there as though I sot in the midst on 'em. And it is the strangest thing in the world, too, that Christian people can act so. There must be some of the love of Christianity wantin' in their hearts, or they could not treat a brother in Christ in that way. As I sot there, I thought, 'can there be any sich place as a dark-hole, or black pew, or behind the door, or under the fence, in heaven? If there is sich a spirit or policy there, I don't feel very anxious desire to go there.' The bible says, 'God is no respecter of persons.'

"And what is worse than all, this spirit is carried to the graveyard; and for fear that the dead body of a black man shall black up or disgrace the body of a white, they go and dig holes round under the fences, and off in a wet corner, or under the barn, and put all of our colour in 'em; for every one may be an eye-witness if he'll go to our graveyard and others; for I have lived now goin' on fourteen years in one place, and any colored person who has been buried at all there, had been buried all along under the fences, and close up to the old barn that stands there. I know God will receive the souls of sich, jist as well as though they was buried in the middle of the yard, but I say this, to let the reader know what a cruel and unholy thing prejudice agin color is, and what it will do to us poor black people.

"Now I know that all this is the reason why the people of our colour don't rise any faster. The scorn, the disgrace that every body flings on 'em, keeps 'em down, and they are sinkin', and such treatment is enough to sink the Rocky mountains.

"Now I know from experience, that the better you treat a black man the better he will behave; for his own pride will keep his ambition up, and he'll try to rise; why if you should treat white folks so they'd grow bad jist as fast. Why, who don't know that a body will try to git the good will of those who treat 'em well, so as to make 'em respect 'em still more? And it's jist like climbin' a ladder; you'll git up a round any day, but if you keep a knockin' a man on the head with the club of prejudice, how in the name of common sense can he climb up.

"Now this is most as bad as slavery; for slavery keeps the foot on the black man's neck all the time, and don't let 'em rise at all; and prejudice keeps a knockin' on him down as fast as he gits up; and we ought not to go to the South, till we can git the people of the North to treat our color like men and women. A good many people oppose abolitionists, and say, 'why what will you do with the niggers when they are free? They will become drunken sots and vagabonds like our niggers at the North; why don't *they* rise?' I can answer that question in a hurry! The reason is, because they don't give us the same chance with white folks; they won't take us into their schools and colleges, and seminaries, and we don't be allowed to go into good society to improve us; and if we set up business they won't patronize us; they want us to be barbers, and cooks and whitewashers and shoeblacks and ostlers, camp-cullimen, and sich kind of mean low business. We ain't suffered to attend any pleasant places, or enjoy the advantages of debating schools and libraries, and societies, &c. &c., and all these things is jist what improves the whites so fast. And if we by hook or by crook git into any sich place, why some feller will step on our toes, and give us a shove, and say, 'stand back nig, you can see jist as well a little furder off.

"Now all these things is what keeps us so much in the back ground; for if we have a chance, we git up in the world as fast as any body. For there *is* smart and respectable colored folks; and you sarch out their history, and you'll find that they once had a good chance to git larnin', and they jumped arter it. I think one of the greatest things the abolition folks should be arter, is to help the free people of color to git up in the world, and grow respectable, and educated, and then we will prove false what our enemies say, 'that we are better off in chains than we be in freedom.'"

ENDNOTE FOR CHAPTER V

i. What a cheerful air hangs around the path of liberty! I was once reading this page to a warm-hearted and benevolent Abolitionist, and when I came to this speech of the captain, he burst into tears as he exclaimed, "Oh, what a change in that boy's existence! It seems to me that such kindness must almost have broken his heart. Oh! a man must have a bad heart not to desire to see every yoke broken, and all the oppressed go free."

BOOK THE SECOND.

PETER WHEELER ON THE DEEP.

CHAPTER I.

Beginning of sea stories—sails with Captain Truesdell for the West-Indies—feelings on leaving the American shore—sun-set at sea—shake hands with a French frigate—a storm—old Neptune—a bottle or a shave—caboose—Peter gets two feathers in his cap—St. Bartholomews—climate—slaves—oranges—turtle—a small pig, "but dam' old"—weigh anchor for New York—"sail ho!"—a wreck—a sailor on a buoy—get him aboard—his story—gets well, and turns out to be an enormous swearer—couldn't draw a breath without an oath—approach to New-York—quarantine—pass the Narrows—drop anchor—rejoicing times—Peter jumps ashore "a free nigger."

Author: "Where do you hail from to day, Peter?"

Peter. "From the street, where I've found some folks that makes me feel bad."

A. "What now, Peter?"

P. "Why, there's some folks that feels envious and flings this in my face—'Oh! you've got to be a mighty big nigger lately, han't ye? and you're a goin' to have your life wrote.' And this comes principally from people of my own colour, only now and then a white person flings in somethin' to make it go glib; but the white folk round here generally treat me very kindly."

A. "Well, don't revenge yourself, Peter; bear it like a man and a christian. Now let us launch out on the deep."

P. Well, we'll weigh anchor,—but it won't do for me to tell every thing that happened to me in my sea v'iges, for 'twould fill fifty books; and so I'll only tell some things that always seemed to please folks more'n the rest:

I followed the North River all that summer I run away, and in the fall of that year Captain John Truesdell sold his sloop and engaged to go out to sea as master of a large vessel for a company of New York merchants.

"So, on the 22d of October, 1806, at nine o'clock we weighed anchor for St. Bartholomews, and bore away for the Narrows. Arter we'd got out some ways, I turned back to take one look at my old native land, and I felt kind'a streaked, and sorry and grieved, and you may say I felt kind'a rejoiced tu, for if I was a goin' away from home and country, out on the wide waters, I'd got my liberty, and was every day gettin' it *stronger.*

"We had a fine ship; she was one of the largest vessels in port, and she carried twenty guns, for she was rigged to sail for any port, and fight our own way. We had thirty-seven able-bodied men besides officers; and in all, with some officers, about fifty men aboard. When we'd been out nearly two days, towards night, we looked off ashore, and the land looked bluer and bluer, till all on it disappeared, and nothin' could be seen but a wide waste of waters, blue as any thing, and the sun set jist as though it fell into a bed of gold; and when the moon riz she looked jist as though she come up out of the ocean; and the next mornin', when the mornin' star rose, he looked like a red hot cinder out of a furnace. Well, *we all looked till we got out of sight of land,* and them some went to cryin' and *I* felt father ticklish; but most on us went to findin' out some amusements. The sails was all filled handsome, and she bounded over the waters jist like a bird. Some on us went to playin' cards, some dice, and some a tellin' stories, and he that told the fattest story was the best feller.

"Next day 'bout nine in the mornin', we spied a French frigate on our larboard bow, bearin' right down upon us, and first she hailed, "ship ahoy!" Captain answered, and the frigate's captain says, "what ship?" "Sally Ann, from New-York." The Frenchman hollered, "drop your peak and come under our lee." And he did, and he come on board our ship with twelve men, and captain took 'em down into the cabin, and hollers for me, and says, 'bring twelve bottles of madeira;" and so I did, and stepped back and listened, and there they talked and jabbered, and I couldn't understand 'em any more'n a parcel of skunk blackbirds; but our captain could talk some French. Well, they stayed aboard I guess, two hours, and examined the ship all through, and then they left, and boarded their ship, and they fired us two guns, and we answered 'em with two stout ones, and then we bore off under a stiff breeze. This is what sailors calls shakin' hands, and wishin' good luck, this firin' salutes.

"The fifth day about ten o'clock A.M. there comes up a tremendous thunder storm, and the waves run mountain high, and it blowed as though the heavens and arth was a comin' together; and the wind and storm riz till two o'clock in the arternoon, and *increased;* and we drew an ile cloth over the hatch comin's and companion way. And all the sails was took down, every rag on 'em, and we sailed under bare poles; and the log was flung out, and we found we was a runnin' at the rate of fifteen knots an hour; and there come a sea and swept every thing fore and aft, and it took me, for I'd just come out of my caboose, and swept my feet right from under me, but I hung fast to the shrouds; and there wave arter wave beat agin us, and swept over us clean. And oh! dear me suz, the lightnin' struck on the water and sissed like hot iron flung in, and the thunder crashed like a fallin' mountain, and the sailors acted some on 'em pretty decent, and the rest on 'em like crazy folks. They ripped, and swore, and cussed, and tore distressedly; and one old feller up aloft reefin' sail, his head was white as flax, cussed his Maker, 'cause he didn't send it harder.

"Oh! how I trembled when I heard him! Why he scart me a thousand times worse than the lightnin'. 'Bout nine at night we tries the pumps, and finds three feet water in the hold, and then eight men went to pumpin' till the pumps sucked, and the captain looked pretty serious I tell ye; and 'bout twelve o'clock the storm went down, and all was quiet, only the sea, and that was distressedly angry; and the next mornin' 'twas as calm, as the softest evenin' ye ever see.

"Captain comes round and says, 'boys, old Neptune will be round to-day, and make every one pay his bottle or be shaved,' and sure enough, 'bout eleven the old feller comes aboard with an old tarpaulin hat on, and his jacket and breeches all tore to strings, and the water running off on him, and says, 'captain you got any of my boys aboard?' 'Yis, here's one;' and he p'inted at *me*. 'Well boy, what have you got for me to day?' 'A bottle of wine,' says I; and he says, 'now I'm goin' to swear you by the crook of your elbow, and the break of the pump, that you will let no man pass without a bottle or a shave.' So he goes round to all on board and then goes away. The captain told me he was 'old Neptune, and lived in the ocean;' but I was detarmined to foller him; so on I goes arter him, and I finds him snug hid under the cathead a changin' his clothes, and then he comes on deck, and I charged him that he was the old Neptune, and finally he confessed it, and said 'twas the way all old sailors did to make every raw hand, when they got to sich a spot in the ocean, pay his bottle or be shaved with tar, soap, and an iron razor.

"Along in the day, captain calls all hands on deck, and says, 'we've had a pretty hard time boys, and now we'll rig a new caboose, and clear up, and then we'll splice the main brace;' and 'twas done quick and well, *for grog was ahead.*

"The captain says to me, 'now cook, you go down and draw that ten quart pail full of wine, and give every man a half a pint; and drink and be merry boys, but let no man get drunk. Well, I got a good supper, and arter that a jollier set of fellers you never seed. We was runnin' under a stiff breeze from N.W. and all sails well filled; and we had sea stories, and songs, and music, and all kinds of amusements, and the captain was as jolly as any body.

"Well, arter bedtime, the captain says, 'cook, you must be my watch to-night,' and he comes and tells me jist how to manage the helm; and he turns in, and I managed it *well,* for I'd managed his old sloop on the river, but this was somethin' more of a circumstance; and afore the watch was up, I got so I could manage a ship as well as the fattest on 'em, and a tickelder feller you never see.

"In the mornin' the hands praised me up; and the captain says, 'why, he's the best man aboard, for he can do *my duty;*' and that made me feel good, and I got two considerable feathers in my cap that time.

"But I must hurry on. We made St. Bartholomews in nineteen days from New York, and sold cargo, and took in a load for Porto Rico, and there filled up with sugar and molasses, and put out for New York. The climate there was hot enough to scorch all the wool off a nigger's head. The fever was ragin' dreadfully in another part of the island, and we didn't, any on us, pretend to go ashore much. The sand was so hot at noon 'twould burn your feet, and the white inhabitants didn't go out at all in the middle of the day; but the niggers didn't seem to mind the heat at all; bare-footed, bare-headed, and half-naked; yis, more'n halt a considerable, and it seemed the hotter it was the better they liked it. But they suffered a god deal, and they'd come aboard our ship and try to make thick with the crew. They talked a broken lingo, kind'a Ginney, I s'pose; and they called white folks 'buddee,' and they'd say, 'buddee give eat, and I give buddee orange.' And so at night, they'd fetch their oranges aboard, and give a heap on 'em for a few sea-biscuit, and I tell ye, them oranges wan't slow. One night, five or six on 'em fetched a big sea turkle aboard, and we bought him and paid a kag of biscuit for him, and he weighed two hundred and seventy pounds, and the feller seemed dreadfully rejoiced, and patted their lips and bellies, and laughed, and kissed the captain's feet, and laughed and seemed tickled enough, and off they went. Next day another feller come aboard, and says, 'Cappy, you buy fat pig?' 'Yis, and when will you bring him?' 'Mornin' Cappy.' So, in the mornin' he come aboard with his pig; he was small, but *terrible fat;* and so the captain pays him and looks at him, and says, 'Jack, your pig is small.' 'Oh! massa, he's small, but *dam old.*' Oh! how the captain laughed! and he used that for a bye-word all the v'yge.

"Well, we cooked the turkle, and sich meat I never see; there was all kinds on it, and if we didn't live fat for some days I miss my guess. I was a goin' to throw the shell overboard, but the captain hollered and stopped me, and so he saved it and sold it in New-York for a good sight of money; and finally, arter bein' in the islands some time, we weighed anchor for New York.

"We'd got 'bout half way home, and one day the cabin boy was aloft, and cries out, 'Sail ho!'

"'Where away?' 'Over the starboard quarter.'

"'How big?' 'As big as a pail of water.'

"'Bear down to her, helmsman, and you cook, bring my big glass.' So I brings it, and 'twas a big jinted thing, and 'twould bring any thing ever so far off as nigh as you pleased. Captain looks and says, 'It's a man on a buoy.' And as we got nearer, sure enough we could see him; and the captain cries, 'down with the small boat, man her strong, put out for him and handle him carefully.' And bein' pretty anxious, I was the first man aboard, and we come along side on him and lifts up his head, and he says in a weak voice, 'Oh! my God! don't hurt me!!' And we lifts him up, and still he hangs to the buoy, and we told him to let go. And he says, 'I will, if you won't let me fall;' and we told him we wouldn't, and he let go reluctantly, and we took him in; and his breast, where he lay on the buoy, was *worn to the bone,* where he'd hugged it, and the motion of the waves had chafed him so. Well, we got him down in a berth, and the captain tries to talk with him, but he couldn't speak, and we changes all the clothes on him that was left, and feeds him with cracker and wine; and the captain sets and feels of his pulse, and says once in a while, 'he's doin' well': and then he fell asleep, and slept an hour as calm as a baby, and the captain told me to wash him in Castile soap-suds, and says he, 'we'll have a new sailor in a hurry.'

I prepares my wash and he wakes up, and says, 'how in the name of God did I come here?' so we told him, and the captain says, 'you hungry?' 'Yis.' And I fed him a leetle more and washed him; and oh! how he swore, it smarted so. 'Where's the captain,' says he. 'Here.' '*Captain, have you got any rum?*' And so he ordered him some weak sling, and arter this he seemed a good deal stronger, and then the captain sets his chair down by him, and asks him who he was and where he come from?

"He says, 'my name is Tom Wilson, and I was born in Bristol, England, and lived there till I was sixteen, and then sailed for Boston, and followed the seas twenty years, and at last was pressed aboard an English man of war in London. I escaped, and got on board a French ship, and started for

America in a merchantman. We'd made 'bout half v'yge when a tremendous storm riz, and we was stove all to pieces, and every body and every thing went down, for all I know, and I took to a big cork buoy as my only hope. The last I see of the wreck was two days arter this. Well, I hung to my buoy, and floated on, and on, and it got calm, and it got to be the fifth day, and I thought I must give up. I lost all sense enemost, and didn't know what did happen, till I heard your boat come up, and then my heart fluttered; and now is the first time for days I know what I am about. And this is the second time I have been cast away and not a man aboard saved but myself. How long I was aboard the buoy arter I lost my sense, I can't say, but it seems to me it was *some* days, but I an't sartin. Now captain, if I get well, make me one of your men.'

"The captain says, 'I will, Tom.'

"Well, he got up fast, and eat up 'most all creation, he was so nigh starved; and when he got able to work ship-tackle, he turns out to be a great sailor, but an awful wicked man, for every breath heaved out an oath.

"Well, in twenty-one days from the West-Indies, we made the New York Light, and then there was rejoicin' enough I tell ye. I know I was glad enough, and as soon as we got hauled up, I jumped ashore and the first thing says I,

"Here's a Free Nigger."

CHAPTER II.

Peter spends the winter of 1806–7 in New-York; sails in June in the Car-napkin for Bristol; a sea tempest; ship becalmed off the coast of England; catch a shark and find a lady's hand, and gold ring and locket in him; this locket, &c. lead to a trial, and the murderer hung; the mother of the lady visits the ship; sail for home; Peter sails with captain Williams on a trad-ing voyage; Gibralter; description of it; sail to Bristol; chased by a pri-vateer; she captured by a French frigate; sail for New-York; Peter lives a gentleman at large in "the big city of New York."

Author. "What did you do in New York, Peter?"

Peter. "We laid by and unrigged for winter, and the captain sent to Troy and had his family brought down to the city, and I lived in his family that winter as servant; and I had fine times tu, for he was a noble man, and lived as independent as a prince, in Broadway, nigh where the Astor House stands. I had a fine winter of it, and come spring he hired the Carnapkin, one of the biggest and best ships in port, and all rigged. We weighed an-chor for Bristol, and this was rare sport for me, for we was a goin' to see old John Bull.

"When we'd been out about seven or eight days, we was overhauled by a tremendous storm from the north-east; and it grew worse and worse, and about midnight she lay on her beam ends for some time, and we expected to go to pieces; and the second mate sounded the hold and found four feet water in her, and that started the hair. We got the pumps agoin' and pretty soon the captain hollers out, 'she rights,' and glad enough we was; and the carpenter found her leak, and makes all tight, and by next day all was clear as a bell. The captain found himself off of his course over two hundred miles, and so he hauls on agin; and in about twenty days we made sight of the white coast of old England, and there we was becalmed for two days, and didn't stir a mile.

"The captain says, 'now boys, you may go and fish till we git a breeze.' Well, we hadn't been out long afore we fell foul of a shark, and the first thing he knowed he had the harpoon in him, and we got him aboard, and then we calculated on a greet hurrah, and sure enough we did have a *melancholy* one tu. The captain says, 'now let's have his liver cooked,' for you see a shark's liver is a great dish at sea. And so I goes to work and cuts him open, and what do you think I found there?

"Why the first thing I found was the *hand of a human person,* and on the middle finger was a gold ring, and on it 'twas wrote who she was in Spanish characters. The captain stands by and says, 'dig carefully a leetle furder and see what you find.' So on I dug with my butcher knife, and up comes a gold chain; and I pulled away and out come a gold locket, and it had a lock of hair in it, and a name on it. We hunted along and found human bones, and nails of fingers partly *dissolved.*

"Well, we made port, and then the captain advertises the story of the shark; and the day arter this there come a splendid carriage to the dock, and who should it be but a Spanish lady, and she was in great splendor tu, and she comes aboard and calls for the captain; and he waits upon her with great respect down into the cabin, and her servant goes down with her, and she spoke in broken English, and asks him all about the shark, and then he tells all about it, and then showed her the hand; and when I brought it she broke out into 'my God!' and she seemed to be grieved and vexed, and broken down, and yit spunky by turns; and then she'd say, as she looked at the locket and hand and ring, 'sacra venga,' and swear, and her face would look red and pale by turns; and finally she turns to the captain and says, 'Sir, this was my child,' and says she 'there was a young Spaniard engaged to my daughter, and they walked out one evening towards the water-side, and that's the last I've heard of my child till now. He went to his own lodgings that night and was inquired of for her, but give no answer, and they made great sarch for her, but nothin' could we hear. It always seemed to me he killed her, but I couldn't git any evidence of it, and so I let it rest, and this happened nearly two weeks ago, and to day, you and your crew must come up and testify to the whole transaction.' So she left.

That arternoon, four gentlemen come in a coach to the ship, and we had to go up to the City Hall, I guess 'twas; a large stone building, and it had great pillars in front on it, and I looked at it *good* I tell you, for 'twas the handsomest buildin' I ever see. So we got there, and they put us all into a room and locked us up; and we stayed there till two o'clock, and then a man come and took out the captain, and then me, and I was sworn, and told the whole story; and then all the crew was fetched on, and testified the same thing; and the cabin-boy, when he finished his testimony, says, 'and I believe this lady was killed and flung overboard by some body,' and he said it with some courage, tu; and at that a young Spaniard of a dark complexion and long black eyebrows that come round under a curl at the corner of his eye, and oh! how black his eye was, and he had long mustaches on his upper lip, and a big pair of whiskers, and I tell you he looked as though he could murder as easy as you could eat a meal of victuals. But he looked kind'a chopfallen, and up he got, and says he, 'I'm the man—I flung her off the wharf, and I give myself up to the law;' you see he had been taken and brought to the bar. Then the king's Attorney Gineral, spoke to this prisoner, and I tell you he was dressed splendidly. He had on an elegant blue coat and satin vest, and black satin pantaloons, and buff pumps, and he had on a girdle of red morocco, and it had a gold plate in front, and it had a big star on it, and his head was powdered in great style, and he fixes his eyes on the Spaniard like a blaze of fire, and says, 'prisoner, deliver up that knife in your sleeve;' and at that the Spaniard slips a ribbon off of his wrist and drew out a knife like what we call a Bowie knife in this country, and handed it to the Attorney, and I tell ye if the Spaniard didn't look beat!

"And then his lawyer got up and made a smart plea for him and set down; but then you might know he was a rowin' agin the tide, for he was a pleadin' for the devil himself.

"Then the Attorney Gineral got up, and says, 'My Lords and Judges, and Gentlemen of the Jury, &c. &c.' And if he didn't make a splendid plea then I'm no judge—I once could tell all about it, for you see I was all ear when them big fellers spoke and we all talked it over on the v'yge so much, and what one forgot, 'tother recollected, and then besides 'twas published in the Bristol papers; and once I say it all to a T, and I only wish I could remember it word for word, it would be sich great stuff for this book. But my memory has kind'a failed me for a few years; only I know the Gineral made all on us cry, he talked so fine, and I do remember the closin' off sayin'. 'My Lords, I have now finished the defence for the crown, and I submit the case to your lordships, feeling that your verdict will respect the rights of the throne and the liberties and safety of its loyal subjects. My Lords I have done.' And down he sat.

"And there that big room—it was as big as the whole of our big red barn—was crowded full as it could stick and hold, and there was a'most all nations on 'arth there. And I tell you if I didn't feel fine to git up afore my lords, (as that ere Attorney Gineral called 'em,) and all them big bugs, and tell about that poor lady there; *and there agin I was treated better than I ever was in an American court in my life; for I never got up in a court room in this country to give testimony or see a black man, who warn't rather laughed at by somebody.* Well, when the Attorney Gineral had finished, three of these 'ere lords I tell on went into another room, and stayed there a few minutes, and come back, and then the chief lord of the establishment got up, and drew on a kind of a black cap, and commanded the attention of all present, and the room was so still you could hear a pin drop. The prisoner was fetched forward, and the Judge turns to him and says:—

"'By the testimony of Captain Truesdell and crew, and by your own confession, I find you, accordin' to the laws of our king and country, *guilty* of this murder; and have you any thing to offer why sentence of death should not be pronounced upon you?' The Spaniard shook his head, and then the Judge pronounced his doom.

"'In the Name of the King of the Realm, and by the Authority of Almighty God, I sentence you to be executed this evening at half-past six o'clock, until you are *dead*, DEAD, DEAD; and may God have mercy on your soul.'

"Well, the sheriff took the prisoner and ordered us to be sent back in a large carriage and four milk white horses to the ship.

Next mornin' at ten o'clock the Spanish lady came aboard, and went down in the cabin with the captain, and sot there and talked a good while about the affair, and cried a good deal, and when she got up she put her hand into her little huzzy and took out twenty doubloons, and give 'em to the captain, and told him to divide that with his crew, and she calls for me and gives me a half-joe, and says she, 'I give you that for bein' so good as to find my darter,' and she went off, and I had a doubloon and a half-joe, and that night we heard the Spaniard was hung.

"Well, we lay in port about four weeks, and we had fine times and see a good many big characters, and I was in England arter this, and I see some of the biggest kind of bugs they got, and I'll tell about that when I git to it. Well, we took in a load of goods, and weighed anchor for home, and had as fine a passage as ever was sailed over the brine. We made New York and the hands was all paid off, and I had one hundred and sixty dollars in specie except a little on the Manhattan Bank. Then I quit Captain Truesdell, and he gin me a recommend, and I hired to Captain James Williams, and we hadn't been in port but four weeks afore I sailed with him for Gauda-loupe. We started in November, on Sunday mornin' jist as the bells begun to ring for church, and weighed anchor for the West Indies, and then I see the difference atwixt the sailor's Sunday and a Yorker's, and it made me feel kind'a serious and rother bad.

"The captain had started on a tradin' and carryin' v'yge; so when we'd cruised round some months in the West Indies, we took a load and sailed for Gibralter, and if that Gibralter warn't a pokerish lookin' place I never see one. We come into the bay and cast anchor under the fort, and they fired three guns over our ship, as a shakin' hands, to let us know we was welcome, and then the captain and officers had to go ashore and account for themselves. As we lay there and looked up, we could see three tiers of cannon one above another, and soldiers with blue coats trimmed with red, and horseskin caps (as I calls them) paradin' there. And as soon as the captain got leave of tradin' back and forth from the governor, all these 'ere cannons was drawn back.

"The English colors way flyin' from the top of the Rock, and at twelve o'clock every day the drums beat, and they played what they called 'The roast beef of old England.' In the mornin' the revelie beat and six cannon was fired from the fort, and if any armed ships lay in the harbor they answered 'em; and every single hour in the night we could hear the sentinel's heavy tread on the Rock, and his cry, ten o'clock and all's well, eleven o'clock and all's well, &c., and so he kept it up all night. Some on 'em told me they'd had distressed times round the old Rock afore this. About the time of our Revolutionary War the French and Spaniards leagued together and got hundreds of ships and thousands of sogers together, and battered away at the old fort, and shot more *red hot* cannon balls agin it than you could shake a stick at; but they only went '*bum, bum,*' and shivered the Rock a little, and fell down into the sea, and they attacked the fort on the land side and worked away there, day arter day, but they didn't hurt a hair of the old Rock's head, and finally they agreed to quit it.—Why Sir, all the nations on the globe could not take that fort. The English will always have it till the eend of the world. Well I looked up through the straits, and it did look beautiful; I could see the African shore; yis, the same Africa where so many millions of my poor brothers and sisters had been stole and carried off into slavery—oh! I felt bad. Well, we sold our load of provisions to the governor of the Rock, and bought a few things and started for England.

"When we'd been out four days we was chased by a privateer, and once they got in a quarter of a mile on us, but we had the most canvass, and we histed the sky scrapers, moon rakers, and star gazers, and water sail, and a good wind. But they fired on us all the time they was near enough. They chased us two days, and then we fell in with a French frigate, and they hailed us, and wanted to know if we'd seen a privateer along the coast, and so the captain told all about it and they gin three cheers and bore away arter her.

"In a few hours we heard a dreadful cannonadin', and a great cloud of smoke riz out of the sea, and we concluded they'd overhauled her, and we left her in good hands. We sailed on for Bristol, and arter we'd been there five days, the news come that a French frigate had captured a Spanish privateer, but didn't take any of her crew, for no sooner than they found themselves taken than they blew up their ship.

"We stayed in Bristol some time, and started at last for New York. On our passage out, we come across a wreck, and we sailed within forty rods on her, and sent out a small boat, and there warn't a livin' soul aboard to tell the story, and there she lay bottom side up, and as handsome a copper bottom as ever you see; but we couldn't do any thing with her, and so we left her and sailed on.

"About a week arter, we was a sailin' along afore a pleasant breeze, and the moon shinin' on the waters, and they looked like melted silver, the first thing we knew up come a seventy-four gun ship right alongside, her guns run out, and men standin' with burnin' torches jist ready to fire, and we felt streaked enough, for we expected to be blown up every minute, and there we stood a tremblin' and didn't dare to say one word; and she passed right by and never fired a pistol, and in one minute she was out of sight—she come and she went and that's all you can say. Now that's what the sailors call '*the phantom ship.*' You see there's no ship about it, only some curious appearances on the sea, that always scares sailors, and makes them think they are a goin' to be captured. Well, we had a fine v'yge home, and made the New York light the first of November, arter a cruise of nearly twelve months. I didn't like Captain Williams, and I quit him, and he paid me off one hundred and fifteen dollars, and I had now two hundred and fifty dollars, and I kept it safe. And a part of the time I went round New York with a saw-buck on my shoulder, and part of the time I was a gentleman at large in the big city—and so I spent that winter.

CHAPTER III.

Peter sails for Gibralter with Captain Bainbridge—his character—
horrible storm—Henry falls from aloft and is killed—a funeral at sea—
English lady prays—Gibralter and the landing of soldiers—a frigate and
four merchantmen—Napoleon—Wellington and Lord Nelson—a slave
ship—her cargo—five hundred slaves—a wake of blood fifteen hundred
miles—sharks eat 'em—Amsterdam—winter there—Captain B. winters in Bristol—Dutchmen—visit to an old battle field—stories about
Napoleon—Peter falls overboard and is drowned, *almost*—make New
York the fourth of July—Peter lends five hundred dollars and loses
it—sails to the West Indies with Captain Thompson—returns to New
York and winters with Lady Rylander—sails with Captain Williams for
Gibralter—fleet thirty-seven sail—cruise up the Mediterranean—Mt.
Etna—sails to Liverpool—Lord Wellington and his troops—war between Great Britain and the United States—sails for New York and goes
to sea no more—his own confessions of his character—dreadful wicked—
sings a sailor song and winds up his yarn.

Peter. "The next spring in the fore part of May, I saw Captain Bainbridge on the Battery, and he hails me and says, 'don't you want a berth
for a summer v'ge?' I says, 'yis Sir,' and then we bargains about wages; and
I was to have twenty-five dollars a month, and he told me to go to the
Custom-house in the mornin'; and so I did, and several others he'd seen,
and we all hired out, and he gin me a steward's perquisites and twenty-five
dollars a month. So we goes aboard his fine new ship jist built in New
Bedford, and 'twas one of the best I ever see; and she was to sail in a week
on Monday, and all on us agreed to be aboard, by ten o'clock; and by ten
o'clock all on us was there to a man, and we received our orders, and they
was mazin' strict, for he was the strictest captain I ever sailed under, but a
fine feller with all—sound, good hearted and a hail feller well met.

"We all hands stood on deck, and a sight of passengers, and we'd bid
our wives and sweethearts all farewell, and at twelve o'clock, noon, we
weighed anchor for Gibralter. The pilot took us out to sea—she was a little
steamboat, for only two or three years afore this, Fulton got his steamboat
invented on the Hudson. Well she left us 'bout three o'clock and bid us
all 'good bye;' and a nice evenin' breeze sprung up, and we spread all sail
and cut the waves like any thing. And so 'bout midnight I goes on deck,
and looked and looked ashore, but the shore of my country was hid, for
we'd moved on so brisk, it had disappeared. We had a beautiful time till

we'd sailed eight days; and one day afterwards the breeze grew stronger, and the moon shone and played over the waters, till it looked like silver; and such an evenin' I hardly ever see be at sea.

"Well next day at one o'clock, a dark awful cloud riz up out of the north-east, and it got so the lightnin' played along the edge of the cloud pretty briskly afore it covered the sun. The thunder rattled like great chariots over a great stone pavement. Captain orders all hands to their posts, and begun to reef and make all fast, and cover the hatches, and prepare for a storm. Finally the cloud covered the whole face of the heavens, and the captain says 'attention all hands! Now fellow sailors be brave, we've got a new ship and her riggin' will slack some, and we don't know how she'll work; but stick to your posts, and by the help of God, we'll weather the storm.'

"Well the storm increased, and we kept a reefin'; for you see I used to be 'bout as much of a sailor as any on 'em, and in a storm there warn't much to be cooked till 'twas over. And I quit the caboose, and was in the riggin' and all round the sap works till it abated. While we was takin' a double reef on the main sail of the mizzen mast, there was a boy by the name of Henry Thomson, the captain's boy, who went up aloft with an old sailor, to larn to take a reef-plat, and by misfortune, one of the foot-ropes gin way, and the little feller *fell* and struck on the quarter-deck railin', and left part of his brains there, and his body went overboard; and we was agoin' so fast, we couldn't 'bout and get him, and we had to leave the poor feller to find companions in the deep. *Oh! he was a noble boy* and I felt so arter it, that I always thought of this varse of an old sailor song.

'Days, months, years, and ages, shall circle away,
And still the vast waters above thee shall roll,
Earth loses thy pattern, for ever and aye,
Oh! sailor boy! sailor boy! peace to thy soul.'

"Well we sailed on, and the storm increased till midnight; and oh! how the ocean did look! It seemed as though it was all ablaze of fire, and the ship couldn't keep still one second. She pitched and tumbled about like a drunken man, and yit every thing held as strong as iron; and so 'bout one o'clock at night, the storm passed off 'bout as quick as it had come, and as soon as any light appeared in the heavens, the captain says, 'cheer up boys! the storm is agoin' over and all hands to *bunk*, only the watch.'

"In the mornin' it was as clear and pleasant as clear could be, only the sea was dreadful rough; for you know it takes the sea a good while to git calm arter a storm; but we gits breakfast and she grows kind'a calmish, and then the captain comes on deck and tells one of the hands to go and git a canvass sack and sow it up, and put a stick in it, and a cannon ball at each eend; and then he orders a plank lashed to the side of the ship, with one eend slantin' down to the water, and calls 'all hands 'tention,' and then asks, 'is there any body aboard that feels as though he could pray?' And it was as still as death, and all looked at one another, and nobody answered; for you see in all that company of 'bout fifty, nobody could pray to his God. And all was awful, for I tell ye what 'tis Domine, it's a pretty creepy feelin' gits hold on a body, if they knows that nobody round 'em can pray!

"But in the suspense there steps out an elderly English lady, and she said 'Let us pray! Oh! thou who stillest the waves, &c.' And so she went on and if she didn't make the best prayer I ever heard afore or since, and she made a beautiful address to us, and she did talk enough to move the heart of a stone, and with tears in her eyes; and she reproved us for *swearin'* so. And while she was a talkin' and prayin' so, there lay the like of that beautiful boy cold in death, and I tell ye it made us *cry some* and *feel a good deal.* Well we made as though we put Henry in that sack, and put him on the plank, and let him slide off into the ocean, and when he sunk it seemed as though my heart went into the sea arter him.

"Well the spot where his brains lay there on the deck, stayed there as long as I stayed aboard that ship; and I used to stand there and watch it at evenin', and cry and cry; and I guess if all the tears I shed had been catched, they'd filled a quart cup; but I couldn't help it, for he was a noble boy, and I loved him like a brother. But we sailed on and left Henry behind us, and the thoughts on him sometimes checked our glee and sin, but only for a little while, and all on board soon forgot him, only me. But oh! how I did love that boy.

"Well we made Gibralter in thirty-six days from New York, and as we lowered sail and cast anchor under the old fort, they fired six cannon over our mast, and the English officer comes aboard, and three of his aids, and the ship and cargo and all her writings was examined, and findin' all right side up, he gin us permission to come ashore and do business; and the governor bought our load of provisions for the navy sarvice, and we got an extra price 'case 'twas *scarce;* and while we lay there, there was four English gun-ships of the line come in freighted with soldiers from Plymouth, in England, and they was under the convoy of Admiral Emmons; and they left their soldiers and took some on the rock, and when they come in sight, if there warn't some music and some smoke. All the instruments used in the English navy was played on the ships, and they fired gun arter gun, from the ships to the fort, and the fort to the ships, and every round they fired, they beat the English revelie, and oh! how them cannon shook the ship under us, and the smoke was so thick, you could fairly cut it; and so they kept it up, and I tell ye they had jolly times enough.

"Next day they begun to land their recruits, rank and file by companies, and as one company from the ship marched up the rock to the top of the fort, another company from the rock would march down aboard the ship, and in this way we see a heap on 'em landed and shipped. And there stood the Royal band all day in plain sight; and they was all colored folks, and *they felt good tu*, and every time they landed they'd fire a broadside from the fort, and shelter 'em with smoke; and every time a company of the fort's soldiers come aboard the ship, they'd cover 'em with smoke; and put it all together, it was by all odds the handsomest sight I ever see in my travels.

"Well, two days arter this, 'bout nine o'clock in the morning, the cannon begun to blaze away from the old fort agin', and we concluded we was agoin' to have some more *doin's*, and I up on deck and looked and looked, and bim'by I see a large frigate comin' up leadin' four merchantmen with flying colors, and she blazed back agin', and when she got into the harbor, the seventy-fours in port opened their mouth agin', and so we had it pretty lively.

"These merchantmen were loaded with provisions for the navy; oh! what a heap of folks there was in that Rock!! Our captain says 'boys, they've bought our cargo, but I don't s'pose 'twould make a mouthful apiece for 'em.' And what an expensive establishment that English army and navy is!

"We stayed there at the Rock a good while, and these merchant vessels went out under the protection of these navy ships, to victual the English fleet there; and we heard a good deal 'bout Napoleon and Lord Wellington. They was all the talk, and Wellington was all the toast; and their armies was a shakin' the whole 'arth, and ships and armies agoin' and comin' all the time; and there Lord Nelson, he was at the head of the English navy, and he was a great toast; and every day the papers would come and fetch stories of battles on land and at sea, till I was sick on 'em as I could be. It seemed to be nothin' but a story of blood all the time; and Europe and all the ocean was only jist a great buryin' and murderin' ground; and, for my part, I never thought much of these 'ere great wholesale murders, as I calls Bonaparte, Wellington, and Lord Nelson, and sich like sort of fellers.

Why, Domine, I should think, from all accounts I heard at the time, and arter it, that they must have killed all of five millions of folks, in all that fightin' agin Napoleon. Oh! it's a cruel piece of business to butcher folks so; and yit, nevertheless, notwithstanding, them same men *was* toasted, *be*-toasted *now* all over the world, and it makes me sick of human natur'; and if I am a black man, I hate to see respectable people act so.

"Finally, arter a long stay, we hauled up anchor for Port Antonio. One day a man aloft cries out 'ship ahoy.' The captain looks through his big glass and says, 'bear down on her helmsman;' and when we got nigh 'nough, the captain hails her; 'what ship?'

"'Torpedo.'

"'What captain?'

"'Trumbull.'

"'Where from?'

"'African coast.'

"'Where bound?'

"'America.'

"'Can I come on board you?'

"'Yes.

"So he bears down and lays too, and I, 'mong the rest, went aboard. The captain treats us very genteel; and when they'd finished drinkin' Captain Trumbull orders the hatch open, and I looked down, and to my sad surprise I see 'twas crowded with slaves. The first thing I see was a colored female, as naked as she was born into the world, and she looked up at me with a pitiful look; and an iron band went round her leg, and then she was locked to an iron bolt that went from one eend of the ship to the other; and *there was five hundred slaves down in that hole;* men, women, and children, all chained down there, and among 'em all not one had a rag of clothes on,—and not a bit of daylight entered, only that hatchway, and then only when they opened it to throw out the dead ones, or else feed 'em; and when I put my head over the hole, a steam come out so strong 'nough to knock down a horse, for there they was in their own filth, and oh! how they did smell. There was several women that had jist had children, and a good many sick, and there they was, and oh! what a sight,—some on 'em was cryin' and talkin' among themselves, but I couldn't understand a word they said; and there was a parcel of leetle fellers, that was from two to ten years old, a runnin' round 'mong 'em, and some on 'em was *dead,* and you could hear the *dyin' groans of others.* Oh! I never did think a body of folks could suffer so and *live*. Why, how do you think they sat? They all sat down with their legs straddled out right up close agin' one another, and they couldn't stir only one arm and hand, *for all else was chained.*

"I felt worse, I 'spose, and it was entirely more heart-rendin' to me, because they was my own species; they warn't only human bein's but *Africans.* Oh! if I didn't hate slavery arter this worse than ever; why! it seemed to me a thousand times worse than it ever did afore, when I was a slave myself.

"Well, the captain said he started with eight hundred, and three hundred had died on the v'yge! and he'd only been out ten days, and that's mor'n one an hour; and that he had to keep one hand in there nigh upon half the time, to knock off the chains from the dead ones, and pitch 'em upon deck; and, says he, I have left a wake of blood fifteen hundred miles; for, no sooner than I fling one out than a shark flies at him and colors all the water with blood in less than one minute; why, says he, 'a shoal of sharks follows our slave ships clear from Africa to America!!' *Oh! my soul, if there is one kind of wickedness greater, and worser, and viler, and more devilish and cusseder than any other, it is sich business.*

"The slave captain asked our captain if he thought he could git into America? He told him he didn't think he could. 'How long do you calculate to be in that business?' says Captain Bainbridge.'

"I can't tell, Sir.'

"'Well,' Sir, says our captain, as he left the ship, 'I advise you to clear up your ship when you git into port, and quit that cussed traffic, and go aboard a merchantman, and be a gentleman.'[i] And he didn't like it nother'![ii] Well, we left, and boarded our own ship; but that scene of blood I couldn't forgit! I could see them poor crutters, for a good many days, in my thoughts and dreams; and sometimes I could see 'em jist as fresh and sorrowful as ever. Hundreds and hundreds of poor slaves, now at the South, are their descendants; and, like enough, you see some on 'em Mr. L—, when you was at the South; and I know how to pity the descendants of them that's fetched over in slave ships, for one of my grandfathers was fetched out in one, as I told you in the beginnin' on my story.

"Well, we made Port Antonio in three weeks, and stayed there thirteen days, and got a cargo, and then the captain says, 'boys, we shall have a rough passage home, if we go this fall, it's so late, for we stayed a good while over the brine, and now who will hold up hands for staying till next spring?'

"So all on us up with both hands, and we hauled up anchor for Amsterdam—that's in the Dutch country—and we made port in four weeks; and when we'd been there 'bout a fortnight, the captain got a letter from his uncle, James Bainbridge, who was in Bristol, and wanted him to come there and winter with him, for he was a sea captain, tu. So he leaves his ship in our hands, and makes the first mate captain, and we had to obey all his orders; and the captain starts and says, 'farewell boys, keep ship safe till you see me, and I'll write to ye often, and let you know how I cut my jib.' And we see no more on him till airly next spring.

"Well, we had all the fun on shore and aboard we could ask for. White and black, we was all hail fellers, well met. We used to have a heap of visiters aboard, to hear 'bout America. We'd have an interpreter to tell our stories, and almost make some of them smoking, thick-skulled Dutchmen b'lieve that America flowed with milk and honey, and that pigs run 'round the streets here with knives and forks in their backs, cryin' out 'eat me.' I used to be a pretty slick darkey for fixin' out a story, tu, and a big one 'bout America; and then some white man would set by my side and put the edge on, and 'twould go without any greasin'; and the captain used to say, always, that if any deviltry was agoin' on, Pete was always sure to have a finger in the pie. Well, we used to talk a considerable 'bout the wars they was a havin' in the old countries, at that time, and they said they could take us up to a place, a few miles from there, where there had been a great battle, sometime afore; and for curiosity, we all went up to see it. Well, we goes, and finds thirty or forty acres, and there wasn't a green thing on it, and 'twas covered with bones and skulls, and all kinds of balls and spikes, and bayonets, and whole heaps of bones, and I guess you never see so melancholy a place in all your life. Oh! it made me sick of war to see thousands and thousands of human bein's a bleachin' on the sand. And it seemed that the ground where that battle was fit, wouldn't let any green thing grow there, and I don't b'lieve any green thing grows there till this day. And there we was, a hearin' every day 'bout Bonaparte, and his killin' his thousands, and his takin' this city and that city, and his conquerin' this gineral and that gineral; but Lord Wellington give him a tough heat on the land, and Lord Nelson on the sea; but the world see *terrible sorry times* for a few years, while that Napoleon was a runnin' his career.

"Well, captain got back to Amsterdam the first of April, and on the fourteenth we weighed anchor for New York. Well, come the sixth day I guess, at evenin' arter I'd done all my work, and was a settin' on the railin' rother carelessly, the boom jibed and struck me on the top of my head, and the first I knew I was pitched head first into the brine. I fell into the wake and swum as fast as I could, and when I riz on the wave I could see the ship and her lights; and then when I went down in the troughs I lost sight of her, and I begun to feel kind'a streakish I tell ye. But pretty soon a rope struck me on the head, and I grabbed and hung on, and the hands aboard drew, and finally I got up pretty near, and the first I knew, and 'bout the last I knew, a wave come and plunged me head first right agin *the starn*, and that made me all jar agin' and I see mor'n fifty thousand stars; but I hung on, and they drawed me up aboard, and when I come fairly tu, the captain comes along and says:—

"'Nig? where you ben?'

"'Ben a fishin', Sir.'

"'Yis, and if you'd come across a good shark, you'd catched a nice fish wouldn't you?'

"And when he spoke 'bout that, it scart me, for I begun to realize my danger, and I begun to be afeard when 'twas tu late, and I trembled jist like a leaf.

"But I'll hurry on. We made the New York light after a long v'yge, and was kept on quarantine a good while, and on the mornin' of the fourth of July, when the bells was a ringin', and the boars was a flyin' through the bay, and the guns from the Battery and Hoboken was a soundin' along the bosom of the Hudson, all independence; and we landed and jumped ashore, and I think I never in all my life felt sich a kind of gush of joy rush through all my soul, as I did when I hear them bells ring, and them guns roar; and this free nigger jumped ashore and celebrated independence as loud as any body.

"The captain paid us all off, and as I left him, I said I'd never go to sea agin, but that didn't make it so; for I hadn't been ashore a month, afore I was off agin with Captain George Thomson. Then I had five hundred dollars—three hundred Spanish mill dollars, and two hundred on the Manhattan Bank, and I had as good a wardrobe of clothes, both citizen's and sailor's as any other feller. Captain Thomson finds out I'd got this money, and says he, 'you better not be a lugging your money round from port, let it out and git the interest on it;' and so he showed me a rich man, Mr. Leacraft, that wanted it, and he gin me two notes of two hundred and fifty dollars, for one and two years, and I counted out my money; and we sailed for the West Indies. Well, we got there and took in a heavy cargo of groceries, and 'bout for home. But 'twas late in the season, and we had cold blusterin' weather, and finally it grew so cold the rain froze on the riggin'; and the captain says, 'we can't make New York,' and the mate says, 'we can; and so we sailed on till we made the New York light, and we was all covered with ice; and the captain says, 'boys we shall git stove to pieces, for we can't manage our riggin', and we must put back.' So we did, into a warmer climate, and in two or three days the riggin' grew limber, and the ice all dropped off, and it grew warmer and warmer, till at last we was in a region like our Ingen summer.

"Well, we'd been out a week, and Captain Woods, north from Bristol hailed us, and asked how the entrance was to New York. Our captain told him he couldn't get in, but he swore he would, and on he sailed, and he'd been gone ten days, and he come back a cussin' and swearin', and had three of his men froze to death. We stay'd out four weeks longer, and was nearly out of provisions, and obliged to make port; and it moderated a leetle, and finally, arter some trouble, we reached home, and a gladder set of fellers you never did see.

"Well, we got paid off, and I jumped ashore, and says I, 'I'll stay here now; and here's what's off to Lady Rylander's, and the rest of the season I'll play the gentleman, for I'm sick of the brine, and I've got money enough to make a dash in the world.' I'd no sooner got ashore, than a friend of mine comes up, and says, 'Pete, you've lost all your money.' 'That can't be possible,' says I. 'Yis, Pete, Leacraft is twenty thousand dollars worse than nothin'. Well, I was thunderstruck, and goes up to see him. Leacraft says, 'to be sure I am Peter, all broke down; but if God spares my life, you shall have every dollar that's your due.'

"But up to this hour I havn't got a cent on it. Captain Thomson tried and tried to git it for me, but all to no purpose; and I grieved and passed sorrowful days and nights I tell ye; for I'd worked in heat and cold, and in all climates and countries for it, and thought now I should be able to begin life right, and 'twas all struck from me at a blow, and 'twas almost like takin' life I tell ye.

"And now I 'spose I took a wrong step.—One day I was in a grog shop with some of my companions, and I took a wicked oath, and flung down my money on the counter to pay for our wine, and says I, 'hereafter, no man shall run away with the price of my labor, and if I have ten dollars, I'll spend, here she goes,' and down went my rhino, and in ten days I had spent all the pay of my last v'yge; and then I goes to Madam Rylander and hires out for sixteen dollars a month as her body sarvant. Not a finer lady ever set foot in Broadway; and she was as pleasant as the noonday sun, and if her sarvants did wrong, she'd call 'em up and discharge 'em, all pleasant, but firm; and she'd encourage me to be economical and good, and I liked her, but I hadn't got my fill of the brine yit, and so I thought I'd out on the waves again. You see I'd been a slave so long that I was jist like a bird let out of her cage, and I couldn't be satisfied without I was a flyin' all the time, and besides there was great talk about a war with John Bull, and I liked it all the better for that; and so I told Lady Rylander I must be off, and she offered me higher wages; but all that wouldn't do; I was bound for the brine and must go.

"I hired out to Captain Williams agin, as steward, for thirty-one dollars a month; and we weighed anchor for St. Domingo; and we took a load of goods from there and started for the Rock of Gibralter once more. On our passage, we was overhauled by an equinoctial storm, and we had a distressed bad time, and it did seem that we must go to the bottom for days. We fell in with a fleet of thirty-seven sail from the West Indies, under the convoy of two English frigates, for London. You see these ships was merchantmen, and the English Admiral had sent out two frigates to protect 'em; for England and France was at war, and they'd seize each other's commerce, and their governments had to protect 'em. When we got in hailin' distance of the frigates, captain cries out, 'how long do you think the storm will last?' 'Can't say—all looks bad now; two of our vessels have gone to pieces, and every soul lost.' And while we was talkin' the seas broke over us like rollin' mountains; we couldn't lay into the wind at all, and we had to let her fly, and we went like a streak of greased lightnin', and we soon lost sight on 'em; and I tell you 'twas a melancholy sight to see *sich a fleet* strugglin' *with sich a tempest;* but we had all we could attend to at home, without borryin' trouble from abroad. But we finally conquered the storm, and dropped anchor under the old fort agin. We lay in the basin two days, and then got liberty from the governor to go up the straits, and we calculated to run up to Egypt, and we cleared the straits and went into the Mediterranean; and then we was on what our college-larnt fellers calls classic ground.

"One day the captain calls me on deck and says, 'Nig, do you see that city up the coast?'

"'Yis, Sir.'

"'Well, that's the spot you sing so much about; now let's have it; strike up, Nig.'

"So up I struck:

"'To Carthagena we was bound,
With a sweet and lively gale,' &c.

"And I was glad enough to see my old port I'd celebrated so long in my songs. Well, we sailed along and had the finest time ever one set of fellers had—the air was as soft as you please, and the islands was as thick as huckkle-berries, and of all kinds and sizes. We sailed on by one island, and then by another, and bim'by Mount Etna hove in sight, while we was a hangin' off the coast of Sicily, and 'twas rocky, and we couldn't hug the shore very close; but we had a fine sight of the volcano; and there was a steady stream of fire and smoke come out of the top of the mountain, and in the night it was a big sight. It flung a kind of flickerin' light over the sea, and we stayed in sight of it some time; and disposed of our load pretty much, and got back to the fort in just eighteen days. We cleared the old Rock the next arternoon; and I said 'good night,' to the old fort, and I hain't seen her from that day to this.

"We sailed round Cape St. Vincent, off the coast of Portugal, and then crossed the Bay of Biscay, O! and passed Land's Eend—up St. George's Channel, and through the Irish Sea, and, on the eighteenth day, dropped anchor in the harbor of Liverpool.

"The captain calculated to stay in Liverpool till spring, for 'twas now November, and trade a good deal, and bring home a heavy cargo of English goods; but for sartin reasons, I'll tell soon, we didn't do it. While we lay in Liverpool, there was some great *doin's,* I tell ye. The English troops, to the amount of some thousands, marched out under Lord Wellington, for foreign sarvice on the continent, and soon arter this Wellington went to fightin' in Spain. Well, they marched out under superior officers, and in the middle of the troops was Wellington's carriage, drawn by six milk-white horses, splendidly caparisoned, and he was in it, and three or four other big lords; and, on each side of the carriage was six officers, on jet black horses, with drawn swords, and they made some noise tu; and I shall remember, to my dyin' day, how Wellington looked.

"But we hadn't been there long afore the captain comes down one night from the city, aboard ship, and calls out to all the crew, and, says he, 'boys there's agoin' to be war betwixt Great Britain and America, and all that wants to clear port to night, and spread our sails for New York, say home!' and we did say home, *in arnest,* and we made all preparation, and 'bout midnight we weighed anchor, and towed ourselves out as still as we could, and I never worked so hard while I was *free* as I did that night, and by day-light we spread all our sails for home, and in four hours we was out of sight of Liverpool. Arter breakfast we all give three cheers, and all hands says, 'now we are bound for home, sweet home!'

"Well, we had been out 'bout four days, and we fell in with Commodore Somebody's ship, that pioneered a fleet of merchantmen for London;

they hailed us, and we answered the signal and passed on, and they let us go by peaceable, without a word of war or peace, on either side; and glad 'nough we was to pass 'em so, and we spread all our sails for America, and felt thankful for every breeze that helped us forward.

"Well, we had a quick passage, and made the New York light, and I never was so glad to see that light-house in my life, for we expected to git overhauled by an English man-of-war or a privateer every day. Well, we got in the last of March, and this was 1812; and well we did, for the first of April an embargo was laid on all the vessels in the ports of the United States, and the nineteenth of June war was declared agin Great Britain, and then the Atlantic was all a blaze of fire.

"Captain Williams quit his ship, and took a privateer, and he tried to git me 'long with him, and I thought I would, for a while, but, finally, I concluded I wouldn't, *for I was too much afeared of them 'ere blue plums that flew so thick across the brine for two or three years.*

"Well, captain went out and was gone thirty days, and come back, and his success was so good that his common hands shared five hundred dollars apiece, and if I'd a gone, I should have had my five hundred dollars back agin; but I'd no idee of going to be shot at for money, like these 'ere fools and gumps that goes down to the Florida swamps, to be shot at all day by Ingens, for eighteen pence a day. Captain met me one day in the street, and says he, 'nig, if you'd only gone with me, you'd a been as big a cuffee now as any on 'em.' I says, 'captain, I don't care 'bout havin' my head shot off of my shoulders; I'm big cuffee 'nough now!'

"Well, I didn't go to sea durin' the war, and afore we got through with that, I got off of the notion of goin' at all, and I concluded I'd spend the rest of my days on 'terra firma,' as I'd been tossed round on the brine long 'nough, and satisfied myself with seein' and travel, and so I stayed, and I han't been out of sight of land ever since.

"But, one dreadful thing happened to me by goin' to sea,—*I got dreadfully depraved;* and I b'lieve there warn't a man on the globe that would swear worse than I would, and a wickeder feller didn't breathe than Pete Wheeler. No language was too vile or wicked for me to take into my mouth; and it did seem to me, when I thought about it, that I blasphemed my Maker almost every minute through the day; and I used to frequent the theatre, and all bad places, and drink till I was dead drunk for days; and nobody can bring a charge agin me for hardly one sin but murder and counterfeitin' that I ain't guilty on. When I thought 'bout it, I used to think it the greatest wonder on 'arth that God Almighty didn't cut me off and strike me to hell, for I desarved the deepest damnation in pardition; and if any man on 'arth says I didn't, why, all I have to say to sich a man is, that he ain't a judge. *Why, as for prayer,* I never thought of sich a thing for years; and as for Sabbath day, I didn't hardly know when it come, only I used to be on a frolic or spree on that day, worse than any other day in the week. As for the bible, why, for years and years I never see one, or heard one read; and I didn't, at that time, know how to read myself a word; and for six years I never had a word said to me 'bout my soul, or the danger of losin' my soul, and I become as much of a heathen as any man in the Hottentot country: and the truth is, no man can make me out so bad as I raly was, *for besides all I acted out,* there was a hell in my bosom all the time, and these outrageous things was only a little bilin' over,—only a few leetle streams that run out of a black fountain-head.

"Oh! Mr. L.—, I don't know what I should do at the judgment day, if I couldn't have a Saviour. I know I shall have a blacker account than a'most any body there, and how can it all be blotted out, except by Christ's blood?

"Why, Sir, you can't tell how wicked sailors generally be. There aint more'n one out of a hundred that cares any thing 'bout religion, and they are head and ears in debauchery and intemperance, and gamblin', and all kinds of sin, and oh! 'twould make your heart ache to hear their oaths. I've seen 'em tremble, and try to pray durin' a dreadful storm, and all looked like goin' to the bottom—for I don't care how heathenish and devilish any body is, if they see death starin' on 'em in the face, and they 'spect to die in a few minutes, he'll cry to God for help—but no sooner than the storm abated they'd cuss worse than ever. Now this was jist my fashion, and if any body says that a man who abuses a good God like that don't desarve to be cut off and put into hell, why then he han't got any common sense.

"But all this comes pretty much from the officers. I never knowed but one sea captain but what would swear sometimes, and most all on 'em as fast as a dog can trot; and jist so sure as our officers swears, the hands will blaspheme ten times worse; and if the captain wouldn't swear, and forbid it on board, his orders would be obeyed like any other orders, *but, as long as officers swears, so long will sailors.*

"But sailors have some noble things about 'em as any body of men. They will always stand by their comrades in the heart of danger or misfortune, or attack; and if a company on 'em are on shore, you touch one you touch the whole; and if a sailor was on the Desert of Arabia, and hadn't but a quart of water, he'd go snacks with a companion. They are sure to have a soft spot in their hearts somewhere, that you can touch if you can git at it, and when they feel, they feel with all their souls. But, arter all, *it's the ruination of men's characters to go to sea,* for they become heathens, and ginerally, ain't fit for sober life arter it, and *ten to one they ruin their souls.*

"But my v'yges are finished, and I'll sing you one sailor's song, and then my yarn is done."

Author. Well, strike up, Peter."

Peter sings:
"THE SAILOR'S RETURN.
"Loose every sail to the breeze,
The course of my vessel improve;
I've done with the toil of the seas,
Ye sailors I'm bound to my love.

Since Solena's as true as she's fair,
My grief I fling all to the wind;
'Tis a pleasing return for my care,
My mistress is constant and kind.

My sails are all filled to my dear;
What tropic birds swifter can move;
Who, cruel, shall hold his career,
That returns to the nest of his love?

Hoist ev'ry sail to the breeze,
Come, shipmates, and join in the song;
Let's drink, while our ship cuts the seas,
To the gale that may drive her along.

I've reached, spite of tempests, the port,
Now I'll fly to the arms of my love;
And, rather than reef I will court,
And win my beautiful dove."

END OF THE SECOND BOOK.

ENDNOTES FOR CHAPTER III

i. All over the world slavery, in all its forms, is repugnant and offensive to noble and generous feeling: and every where, in all ages and nations, oppression and this unholy traffic meet with a just rebuke. Man's better feeling will revolt from cruelty and injustice until they are extinguished.

ii. Of course he didn't "like it." It never did please the devil to be reproved of his evil deeds. It don't please Southern soul-dealers and soul-drivers to be rebuked.

BOOK THE THIRD.

PETER WHEELER AT THE CROSS.

Dear Friends:

I inscribe this Book to you, for several reasons. I love you, and feel anxious to have you become intelligent and virtuous. I know that there are only a few books adapted to your taste and acquirements; and I have had my eye upon your good in writing this history. I have thought you would understand it a great deal better if it was told in Peter's own language, and so I wrote it just as he told it. I hope you will read it *through,* and follow Peter to the Lamb of God who taketh away the sin of the world. And if you are oppressed by the strong arm of power, and kept down by an unholy and cruel prejudice, forget it and forgive it all, and go to that blessed Redeemer who came to save your souls, that he might clothe you, at last, with clean white linen, which is the righteousness of the saints.

Your friend,

THE AUTHOR.

CHAPTER I.

Lives at Madam Rylander's—Quaker Macy—Susan a colored girl lives with Mr. Macy—she is kidnapped and carried away, and sold into slavery—Peter visits at the "Nixon's, mazin' respectable" colored people in Philadelphia—falls in love with Solena—gits the consent of old folks—fix wedding day—"ax parson"—Solena dies in his arms—his grief—compared with Rhoderic Dhu—lives in New Haven—sails for New York—drives hack—Susan Macy is redeemed from slavery—she tells Peter her story of blood and horror, and abuse, and the way she made her escape from her chains.

Author. "Well, Peter, what did you go about when you quit the seas?"

Peter. "The year I quit the seas, I went to live with Madam Rylander, and stayed with her a year, and she gin me twenty-five dollars a month, and I made her as slick a darkey as ever made a boot shine, and she was as fine a lady as ever scraped a slipper over Broadway. While I lived there, I used to visit at Mr. John Macy's, a rich quaker who lived in Broadway, across from old St. Paul's. There was a colored girl lived with his family, by the name of Susan, and they called her Susan Macy; she was handsome and well edicated tu, and brought up like one of his own children; and they thought as much on her as one of their daughters, and she was a lovely a dispositioned gal as ever I seed; and I enjoyed her society *mazinly.*

"Well, one mornin' she got up and went to her mistress' bedroom, and asked her what she'd have for breakfast—'Veal cutlet' says she; and the old man says, 'Thee'll find money in the sideboard to pay for it;' and she did, and took her basket and goes to the market a singin' along as usual—she was a great hand to sing; and gits her meat, and on her return, she meets a couple of gentlemen, and one had a bundle, and says he, 'Girl if you'll take this bundle down to the wharf, I'll give you a silver dollar; and she thought it could do no harm, and so she goes with it down to the ship they described, and as she reached out the bundle, a man catched her and hauled her aboard and put her down in the hole.

"Her master and mistress got up and waited and waited, and she didn't come; and they went and sarched the street, and finds the basket, but nothin' could be heard of Susan in the whole city; and they finally gin up that she was murdered.

"Well, I'll tell you the rest of the story, for I heard on her arter this.

"I stayed my year out with Madam Rylander, and then I quit; and she

was despod anxious to keep me, but I had other fish to fry, and took a notion I'd drive round the country and play the gentleman.

"I come across, in New York, a young feller of color, his parents very respectable folks who lived in Philadelphia; and they took an anxious notion for me to go home with 'em; and I started with 'em for Philadelphia;
and I had as good clothes as any feller, and a considerable money, and I
thought I might as well spend it so as any way. Well come to Philadelphia,
I found the Nixon's very rich and *mazin' respectable;* and I got acquainted
with the family, and they had a darter by the name of *Solena,* and she was
dreadful handsome, and she struck my fancy right off the first sight I had on
her. She was handsome in fetur and pretty spoken and handsome behaved
every way. Well I made up my mind the first sight I had on her, I'd have
her *if I could git her.* I'd been in Philadelphia 'bout a week, and I axed her
for her company, and 'twas granted. I made it my business to wait on her,
and ride round with her, and visit her *alone,* as much as I could. The old
folks seemed to like it *mazinly,* and that pleased me, and I went the *length
of my rope, and felt my oats tu.* I treated her like a gentleman as far as I knew
how—I took her to New York three times, in company with her brothers and their sweethearts; and we went in great splendor tu, and I found
that every day, I was nearin' the prize, and finally I popped the question,
and arter some hesitation, she said, 'Yis, Peter.' But I had another Cape to
double, and that was to git the consent of the old folks; and so one Sunday evenin', as we was a courtin' all alone in the parlor, I concluded, a faint
heart never won a fair lady; and so I brushes up my hair, and starts into the
old folks' room, and I right out with the question; and he says.

"'What do you mean, Mr. Wheeler?'

"'I mean jist as I say, Sir! May I marry Solena.'

"'Do you think you can spend your life happy with her?'

"'Yis, Sir.'

"'Did you ever see any body in all your travels, you liked better?'

"'No, Sir! She's the apple of my eye, and the joy of my heart.'

"'I have no objection Mr. Wheeler. Now Ma, how do you feel?'

"'Oh! I think Solena had better say, Yis.'

"And then I tell ye, my heart fluttered about in my bosom with joy.

"'Oh, love 'tis a killin' thing;
Did you ever feel the pang?'

"So the old gentleman takes out a bottle of old wine from the sideboard, and I takes a glass with him, and goes back to Solena. When I

comes in, she looks up with a smile and says, 'What luck?' I says, 'Good luck.' I shall win the prize if nothin' happens! and now Solena you must go in tu, and you had better go in while the broth is hot. So she goes in, pretty soon she comes trippin' along back, and sets down in my lap, and I says, 'what luck?' and she says 'good.' So we sot the bridal day, and fixed on the weddin' dresses, and so we got all fixin's ready and even the Domine was spoke for. And one Sabba-day arter meetin', I goes home and dines with the family, and arter dinner we walked out over Schuylkill bridge, and at evenin' we went to a gentleman's where she had been a good deal acquainted; and there was quite a company on us, and we carried on pretty brisk. She was naturally a high-lived thing, and full of glee; and she got as wild as a hawk, and she *wrestled* and scuffled as gals do, and got all tired out, and she come and sets down in my lap and looks at me, and says, 'Peter help me;' and I put my hand round her and asked her what was the matter, and she fetched a sigh, and groan, and fell back and died in my arms!!! A physician come in, and says he, 'she's dead and without help, for she has burst a blood-vessel in her breast.' And there she lay cold and lifeless, and I thought I should go crazy.

"She was carried home and laid out, and the second day she was buried, and I didn't sleep a wink till she was laid in the grave; and oh! when we come to lower her coffin down in the grave, and the cold clods of the valley begun to fall on her breast, I felt that my heart was in the coffin, and I wished I could die and lay down by her side.

"For weeks and months arter her death, I felt that I should go ravin' distracted. I couldn't realize that she was dead; oh! Sir, the world looked jist like a great dreadful prison to me. I stayed at her father's, and for weeks I used to go once or twice a day to her tomb, and weep, and stay, and linger round, and the spot seemed sacred where she rested.

"Well, I stayed in Philadelphia some months arter this, and I tell ye I felt as though *my all* was gone. I stood alone in the world, as desolate as could be, and I determined I never would agin try to git me a wife. It seemed to me I was jist like some old wreck, I'd seen on the shore.

A. "Peter, you make me think of Walter Scott's description of Rhoderic Dhu, in his 'Lady of the Lake.'

"'As some tall ship, whose lofty prore,
Shall never stem the billows more,
Deserted by her gallant band,
Amid the breakers lies astrand;
So on his couch lay Rhoderic Dhu,

And oft his feverish limbs he threw,
In toss abrupt; as when her sides
Lie rocking in the advancing tides
That shake her frame with ceaseless beat
But cannot heave her from her seat.
Oh! how unlike her course on sea,
Or his free step, on hill and lea.'

P. "Yis, Sir! I was jist like that same Rhoderic; what'de call him? Oh! I was *worse*, the world was a prison to me, and I wanted to lay my bones down at rest by the dust of Solena. I finally went back to New York, and stayed there for a while, and then up to New Haven, and stayed there two months, in Mr. Johnson's family; and we used to board college students; and we had oceans of oysters and clams; and New Haven is by all odds the handsomest place I ever see in this country or in Europe; and finally I sailed back to New York, arter tryin' to bury my feelin's in one way and another. But in all my wanderin's, *I couldn't forget Solena.* She seemed to cling to me like life, and I'd spend hours and hours in thinkin' about her, and I never used to think about her without tears.

"Well, I thought I would try to bury my feelin's and forgit Solena, and so I hires out a year to Mr. Bronson, to drive hack, and arter I'd been with him a few months, I called up to Mr. Macy's, my Quaker friend, and I felt kind'a bad to go there tu and not find Susan, for I had the biggest curiosity in the world to find out where she'd departed tu; but I thought I'd go and talk with the old folks, and see if they'd heard any thing about Susan.

"Well, I slicks up and goes, and pulls the bell, and who should open the door but *Susan herself.*

"I says, 'my soul, Susan, how on 'arth are you here? I thought you was dead.' And she says as she burst into tears, 'I have been *all but* dead. Come in and set down, and I'll tell you all about it.'

"I says, 'my heavens! Susan where have you been and how have ye fared?'

"She says, 'I've been in *slavery,* and fared hard enough;' and then she had to go to the door, for the bell rung; and agin pretty soon she comes back and begins her story, and as 'taint very long, and pretty good, I'll tell it, and if you're a mind to put it in the book you may, for I guess many a feller will be glad to read it.

"'Well,' begins Susan, 'I went down to the vessel, to carry a bundle, and *three ruffins seized hold on me,* and I hollered and screamed with all my might, and one on 'em clapped his hand on my face, and another held me down, and took out a knife and swore if I didn't stop my noise *he'd stick it through my heart;* and they dragged me down into the hold, where there was seven others that had been stole in the same way; and these two fellers chained me up, and I cried and sobbed till I was so faint I couldn't set up. Along in the course of the forenoon they fetched me some coarse food, but I had no appetite, and I wished myself dead a good many times, for I couldn't git news to master. I continued in that state for two or three days, and found no relief but by submitting to my fate, and I was doleful enough off, for I couldn't see sun, moon, or stars, for I should think two weeks; and then a couple of these ruffins come and took me out into the forecastle, and my companions, and they told me all about how they'd been stole; and we was a miserable a company as ever got together. Come on deck, I see five *gentlemen,* and one on 'em axed me if I could cook and wait on gentlemen and ladies, and I says 'yis, Sir,' with my eyes full of tears, and my heart broke with sorrow; and he axed me how old I was? I says, 'seventeen,' and he turns round to the master of the vessel and says, 'I'll take this girl.' And he paid four hundred and fifty dollars for me, and he took me to his house; and I found out his name was Woodford, and he told me I was in Charleston; but I couldn't forgit the happy streets of New York. Now I gin up all expectation of ever seein' my own land agin', and I submitted to my fate as well as I could, but *'twas a dreadful heart-breakin' scene. Master was dreadful savage, and his wife was a despod cross ugly woman.* When he goes into the house he says to his wife, 'now I've got you a good gal, put that wench on the plantation.' And he pointed to a gal that had been a chambermaid; and then turnin' to me says, 'and you look out or you'll git there, and if you do *you'll know it.'*

"I'd been there four or five weeks, and I heard master makin' a despod cussin' and swearin' in the evenin', and I heard him oversay, 'I'll settle with the black cuss to-morrow; I'll have his hide tanned.'

"So the next day, arter breakfast, mistress orders me down into the back yard, and I found two hundred slaves there; and there was an old man there with a gray head, stripped and drawed over a whipping-block his hands tied down, and the big tears a rollin' down his face; and he looked exactly like some old gray headed, sun-burnt revolutioner; and a white man stood over him with a cat-o'-nine-tails in his hand, and he was to give him one hundred lashes. And he says, 'now look on all on ye, and if you git into a scrape you'll have this cat-o'-nine-tails wrapped round you;' and then he begun to whip, and he hadn't struck more'n two or three blows, afore I see the blood run, and he was stark naked, and his back and body was all over covered with scars, and he says in kind'a broken language, 'Oh! massa don't kill me.' 'Tan his hide,' says master, and he kept on whippin', and the old man groaned like as if he was a dyin', and he got the hundred lashes, and then was untied and told to go about his work; and I looked at the block, and it was kivered with blood, and that same block didn't git clear from blood as long as I stayed there.

"'Well, this spectacle affected me so, I could scarcely git about the house, for I expected next would be my turn; and I was so afraid I shouldn't do right I didn't half do my work.

"'It wore upon me so I grew poor through fear and grief. I would look out and see the two hundred slaves come into the back year to be fed with rice, and they had the value of about a quart of rice a day, I guess.

"'Every day, more or less would be whipped till the blood run to the ground; and every day fresh blood could be seen on the block,—and what for I never found out, for I darn't ax any body, and I had no liberty of saying any thing to the field hands.

"'I used often to look out of the window to see people pass and re-pass, and see if I couldn't see somebody that I knew; and I finally got sick, and was kept down some time, and I jist dragged about and darn't say one word, for I should have been put on the *plantation for bein' sick!* and I meant to do the best I could till I dropped down dead; but the almost whole cause on it was grief, and the rest was cruel hardship. Well, things got so, I thought I must die soon, and in the height of my sorrow, I looked out and see Samuel Macy—Master Macy's second son, walkin' along the street, and I could hardly believe my eyes; and I was standin' in the door, and I catches the broom, and goes down the steps a sweepin', and calls him by name as he comes along, and I tell him a short story, and he says 'I'll git thee free, only be patient a few weeks.' I neither sees nor hears a word on him for over four weeks, but I was borne up by hope, and that made my troubles lighter. Well, in about four weeks, one day, jist arter dinner, there comes a gentleman and raps at the front door, and I goes and opens the door, and there stood old Master Macy, and I flies and hugs him, and he says 'how does thee do, Susan?' I couldn't speak, and as soon as I could I tells my story; and Master Macy then speaks to mistress, who heard the talk and had come out of the parlor, and says, 'this girl is a member of my family, and I shall take her,' and then master come in and abused Master Macy dreadfully; but he says, 'come along with me, Susan;' and, without a bonnet or anything on to go out with I took him by the hand, and went down to the ship; and, afore I had finished my story, an officer comes and takes old Master Macy, and he leaves me in the care of his son Samuel, aboard, and he was up street about three hours, tendin' a law-suit, and then he come back, and about nine o'clock that evenin' we hauled off from that cussed shore, and in two weeks we reached New York, and here I am, in Master Macy's old kitchen.

"'Well, he watches for this slave ship that stole me, and one day he come in and said he had taken it, and had five men imprisoned; and the next court had them all imprisoned for life, and there they be yit. And now there's no man, gentle or simple, that gits me to do an arrant out of sight of the house. *Bought* wit is the best, but I bought mine dreadful dear. When I got back the whole family cried, and Mistress Macy says,

"'Let us rejoice! for the dead is alive, and the lost is found.'"

CHAPTER II.

Kidnappin' in New York—Peter spends three years in Hartford—couldn't help thinkin' of Solena—Hartford Convention—stays a year in Middletown—hires to a man in West Springfield—makes thirty-five dollars fishin' nights—great revival in Springfield—twenty immersed—sexton of church in Old Springfield—religious sentiments—returns to New York—*Solena again*—Susan Macy married—pulls up for the Bay State again—lives eighteen months in Westfield—six months in Sharon—Joshua Nichols leaves his wife—Peter goes after him and finds him in Spencertown, New York—takes money back to Mrs. Nichols—returns to Spencertown—lives at Esq. Pratt's—Works next summer for old Captain Beale—his character—falls in love—married—loses his only child—wife helpless eight months—great revival of 1827—feels more like gittin' religion—"One sabba'day when the minister preached at me"—a resolution to get religion—how to become a christian—evening prayer-meeting—Peter's convictions deep and distressing—going home he kneels on a rock and prayed—his prayer—the joy of a redeemed soul—his family rejoice with him.

Peter. "Well, I sot a hearin' Susan's story till midnight, and that brought back old scenes agin, and there I sot and listened to her story till I had ene'most cried my eyes out of my head, and I have only gin you the outline. And that kidnappin' used to be carried on that way in New York year after year, and it's carried on yit.[i] Why, they used to steal away any and every colored person they could steal, and this is all carried on by northern folks tu, and it's fifty times worse than Louisiana slavery.

"Well, I stayed in New York till my time was out, and then went to Hartford and worked three years, and enjoyed myself pretty well, *only I couldn't help thinkin' 'bout Solena*. She was mixed up with all my dreams and thoughts, and I used to spend hours and hours in thinkin' about what I'd lost. But arter all I suffered, I'm kind'a inclined to think 'twas all kind in God to take her away, for arter this, I never was so wicked agin nigh. I hadn't time or disposition to hunt up my old comrades, and if any time I begun to plunge into sin, then the thought of Solena's memory would come up afore me and check me in a minute, but I was yit a good ways from rale religion.

"While I was there, in December, 1814, the famous Hartford Convention sot with closed doors, and nobody could find out what they was about, and every body was a talkin' about it, and they han't got over talkin' about it, and I don't b'lieve they ever will. The same winter the war closed and peace was declared. I could tell a good many stories about the war, but I guess 'twould make the book rather too long, and every body enemost knows all about the last war.

"Well, I went down to Middletown and stayed a year there, and then I went to hire out to a man in West Springfield, and he was a farmer, and he hadn't a chick nor child in the world, and he had a share in a fishin' place on the Conecticut, and he was as clever as the day is long. He let me fish nights and have all I got, and sometimes I've made a whole lot of money at one haul, and in that season I made thirty-five dollars jist by fishin' nights, besides good wages—and I didn't make a dollar fishin' for Gideon Morehouse nights for years!

"While I was there a Baptist minister come on from Boston and preached some time, and they had a great revival, and I see twenty immersed down in the Connecticut, and 'twas one of the most solemn scenes that ever I witnessed.

"They went down two by two to the river, and he made a prayer and then sung this hymn, and I shan't ever forget it, for a good many on 'em was young.

"'Now in the heat of youthful blood,
Remember your Creator God;
Behold the months come hastening on
when you shall say 'my joys are gone.'

"And then he went in and baptized 'em; and I know I felt as though I wished I was a christian, for it seemed to me there was somethin' very delightful in it, and then they sung and prayed agin, and then went home.

"Arter this I lived in Old Springfield and was sexton of the church there; and while I rung that bell I heard good preachin' every Sunday, and I larnt more 'bout religion than I'd ever knowed in all my life. I begun to feel a good deal more serious and the need of gettin' religion.

"Arter my time was out there, I went down to New York, and there I met Solena's brother, and that brought every thing fresh to mind agin, and for weeks agin I spent sorrowful hours. I thought I had about got over it and the wound was healed; but then 'twould git tore open agin and bleed afresh, and sorrowful as ever. It did seem to me that nothin' would banish the image of that gal from my heart.

"I used to call and see Susan Macy occasionally, and she was now Mrs. Williams, and lived in good style tu, for a colored person. She was married at Mr. Macy's and they made a great weddin', and all the genteel darkies in New York was there; and I wan't satisfied with waitin' on *one,* I must have *two,* and if we didn't have a stir among our color about them times I miss my guess; and Mr. Macy set her out with five hundred dollars, and she had a fine husband and they lived together as comfortable as you please.

"Now I concluded I'd quit the city for good, I spent more money there and had worse habits, and besides all this I wanted to git away as fur as I could from the scene of my disappintment.

"Well, I pulled up stakes agin and put out for the Bay State agin, and I put into Westfield, and stayed there eighteen months, and made money and saved it, and behaved myself, and 'tended meetin' every sabba'day, and gained friends and was as respectable as any body. From Westfield I went to Sharon and there I stayed six months, and 'tended a saw mill, and there was a colored man there by the name of Joshua Nichols, who had married a fine gal, and he lived with her till she had one child and then left her, and went out to Columbia county, New York; and I started off for Albany, and she axed me if I wouldn't find her husband on my route, and so I left Sharon and got here to Spencertown, and found him, and axed him why he would be so cruel as to leave his wife? He says, 'if you'll go and carry some money and a letter down to her I'll pay you.' So he gin me the things and I put out for Sharon, and when Miss Nichols broke open the letter she burst into tears, and says I, "why Miss Nichols what's the matter?" "Why Joshua says this is the last letter I may ever expect from him."—Well, I stayed one night, and come back and concluded I'd go on for Albany, but when I got to Erastus Pratt's he wanted to hire me six months, and I hired, and his family was nice folks, and he had a whole fleet of gals—and they was all as fine as silk, but I used to tell Aunt Phebe, that Harriet was the rather the nicest—on 'em all. Arter my six months was out, I worked a month in shoein' up his family, and I guess like enough some on 'em may be in the garret yet.

"Next summer I hired out to old Capt. Beale, and he was a noble man, and did as much for supportin' Benevolent Societies as any other man in town, and in the mean time, I had got acquainted with her who is now my wife, and this summer I was married to her by Esq. Jacob Lawrence, and in the winter we went to keepin' house.

"When we had been married over a year, we had a leetle boy born, and the leetle feller died and I felt bad enough, for he was my only child, and it was despod hard work too, to give him up. I had at last found a woman I loved, and all my wanderings and extravagancies was over, and I was gettin' in years, and I thought I could now be happy and enjoy all the comforts of a home and fireside, but this was all blasted when I laid that leetle feller in the grave, and my wife was sick and helpless eight months.

"In 1827 a great Revival spread over this whole region, and was powerful here, and I used to go to all the meetin's, and I begun to think more about religion than I ever did in all my life; and these feelin's hung on to me 'bout a year, and agin I gin myself up to the world, and plunged into sin, and grieved the Spirit of God, and grew dreadful vile, as all the folks 'round here will say, if you ax 'em.—And I myself, who knows more 'bout myself than any other body, s'pose that *at heart*, I was one of the wickedest men in the world.

"Well, along in 1828 the religious feelin' 'round in this region, begun to rise agin 'round in this neighbourhood, and there was a good many prayer meetin's held, principally at Deacon Mayhew's, and Esq. Pratt's, and I used to 'tend 'em pretty steady, and I got back my old *feelin'* agin, and now felt more a good deal like gittin' religion, than I ever had; and rain or shine, I'd be at the meetin's, and I determined I'd go through it, if I went at all. This church here, which has since got so tore and distracted, was all united, and seemed to be a diggin' all the same way, and Christ was among 'em. *There was one Sabbath day, I shan't ever forgit,* and when I went to meetin', and the minister took his text "Turn ye, turn ye, for why will ye die?" the very minute the words come out of his mouth, an arrow went to my heart, and I felt the whole sarmint was aimed at me, and I felt despod guilty. I went home, and that night I was distressed beyond all account, and I went to bed troubled to death. But I formed the resolution, if there was any thing in religion I'd have it, if I could git it, and I was detarmined as I could be that I would hunt for the way of Salvation; and when I found it, I travelled in it, and consider that there I *begun right.* But I was ignorant of rale religion as a horse-block, and I didn't know how to go to work. Sometimes, something would say, 'Oh! Peter, give up the business, you can't git it through,' but I held to my resolution *despod tight;* and I think, that is the way for a body to go about getting religion; on the start, be detarmined to hunt for the path of duty, and as soon as you find it, go right to travellin' on it, and keep on; I knew I had some duty to do to God, and I knew I must hunt for it if I found it, and *do* it if I ever got the favor of God.

"Well, one night there was a prayer meetin' in the church, and a shower of prayer come down on the house like a tempest, and oh! how they did beseech God that night—as the Bible says, "with strong cryin' and tears.""

"Deacon Mayhew got up and says, "There's full liberty for any body to git up and speak or pray." And I felt as though I must git up and say somethin' or pray, I was so distressed; but then I was a black man, and was afeard I couldn't pray nice enough, and so I set still, but I felt like death. A number of young converts, prayed and made good prayers, and there was a despod feelin' there I tell ye.

"Arter meetin' a good many folks spoke to me, but I couldn't answer 'em for tears; and so I started for home, when I was goin' cross the lots a cryin' I come to a large flat rock, and looked round to see if any body was near by, and then I kneeled down and 'twas the *first time I ever raly prayed.*

"I begun, but I was so full I couldn't only say these words and I recollect 'em well.

"'Oh! Lord, here I be a poor wretch; do with me just as you please; for I have sinned with an out stretched arm, and I feel unworthy of the least marcy, but I beg for *blood,* the blood of him that died Calvary! Oh! help me, keep up my detarmination to do my duty, and submit to let you dispose on me jist as you please, for time and eternity; oh! Lord hear this first prayer of a hell-desarving sinner.'"

"Well, I got up, and felt what I never felt afore; I felt willing to do God's will, and that I was reconciled to God; afore this, I had felt as though God was opposed to me, and I'd got to shift round afore he'd meet me, and feel reconciled to me. I looked up to heaven, and I couldn't help sayin', 'My Father:' never before nor sence, have I felt so much joy and peace as I felt then. I was glad to be in God's hands, and let him reign, for I knew he would do right, and I felt sich a love for him, as I can't describe.

"I got up from the rock, and the world did look beautiful round me; the moon shone clear, and the stars, and then I thought about David, when he tells about his feelin's when he looked at the same moon and stars; you see I was changed and that made the world look so new; and this beautiful world was God's world, and God was *my Father,* and that made me happy, and that is 'bout all I can say 'bout it.

"I went home, and found my wife and mother-in-law abed and 'sleep, and I lit up the candle and wakes 'em up, and says,

"'I've found the pearl of great price.'

"I gits down the New Testament, for I had no Bible, and never owned one till this time, and says, "I'll read a chapter and then make a prayer, (for you see my wife had larnt me to read arter a fashion,) and they say 'That's right Peter, I'm glad you feel as though you could pray,' I opened the Testament to the 14th chapter of John, 'Let not your heart be troubled; ye believe in God, believe also in me,' &c. Then I made a prayer and set up my family altar, and I have prayed in my family every day, and mean to keep it up, for I believe all christians ought to pray mornin' and evenin' in their families.

"Well, I went to bed and talked to my wife 'bout religion, till I fairly talked her asleep, and then I lay awake and thought, and prayed, and wept for joy, and it will be a good while afore I forgit that night.

"For who can express
The sweet comfort and peace
Of a soul in its arliest Love."

END.

ENDNOTE FOR CHAPTER II

i. It became so common in New York that there was no safety for a colored person there, and philanthropy and religion demanded some protection for them against such a shocking system.—At last there was a vigilance committee organized for the purpose of ascertaining the names and residences of every colored person in the city; and this committee used regularly to visit all on the roll, and almost every day some one was missing. The result has been that several hundreds of innocent men and women and children have been retaken from their bondage, from the holds of respectable merchantmen in New York, to the parlours of southern gentry in New-Orleans. The facts which have been brought out by this committee are awful beyond description.—It is one of the noblest, and most patriotic and efficient organization on the globe. But their design expands itself beyond the protection and recovery of kidnapped friends;—it also lifts a star of guidance and promise upon the path of the fugitive slave; it helps him on his way to freedom, and not one week passes by without witnessing the glorious results of this humane and benevolent institution, in the protection of the free or the redemption of the enslaved. The Humane Society, whose object is to recover to life those who have been drowned, enlists the patronage and encomiums of the great and good, and yet this Vigilance Committee are insulted and abused by many of the public presses in New York, and most of the city authorities.—Why? Slavery has infused its deadly poison into the heart of the North.

Notes

1. Charles Lester, *A Farewell Discourse: Delivered before the Congregation of St. Peter's Church in Spencertown, New York* (New York: W. Dean, 1838); for revival, see *New York Evangelist,* September 12, 1836. For "negro pew," see *Colored American,* November 4, 1837. For pew assignment and early history of the church, see *Columbia County at the End of the Century* (Hudson: Record Printing and Publishing, 1900), vol. 2: 708–09. On divisions among Presbyterians, see John R. McKivigan, *The War against Proslavery Religion: Abolitionism and the Northern Churches* (Ithaca, NY: Cornell University Press, 1984).

2. Vernon Loggins, *The Negro Author: His Development in America* (New York: Columbia University Press, 1931), 99–100. For later studies, see Charles T. Davies and Henry Louis Gates Jr., eds. *The Slave's Narrative* (New York: Oxford University Press, 1985), and Charles H. Nichols, *Many Thousand Gone: The Ex-Slaves' Account of Their Bondage Freedom* (Bloomington: Indiana University Press, 1969).

3. On new styles for the 1840s, see William L. Andrews, *To Tell a Free Story: The First Century of Afro-American Autobiography, 1760–1865,* (Urbana: University of Illinois Press, 1986), 99–102. For a discussion of northern slave narratives, see Graham Russell Hodges, ed., *Black Itinerants of the Gospel: The Narratives of John Jea and George White* (Madison, WI: Madison House, 1993).

4. See John W. Blassingame, "Using the Testimony of Ex-Slaves: Approaches and Problems," in Davies and Gates, *Slave's Narrative,* 78–98.

5. Leah Blackman, *History of Little Egg Harbor Township, Burlington County, New Jersey, from Its First Settlement to the Present Time* (ca. 1880; Tuckertown, NJ: Great John Mathis Foundation, 1963), 192–93, 223, 231; *Tax Ratables for Little Egg Harbor,* Book 203, p. 270, Reel 3 (Burlington County), New Jersey Department of State and Archives, Trenton.

6. Major E. M. Woodward and John F. Hageman, *History of Burlington and Mercer Counties, New Jersey, with Biographical Sketches of Many of Their Pioneers and Promi-*

nent Men (Philadelphia: Everts and Peck, 1883), 226–30, 334, 340–43; John H. Barber and Henry Howe, *Historical Collections of the State of New Jersey* (New York: S. Tuttle, 1844), 107–09; Francis Bazley Lee, *Genealogical and Memorial History of the State of New Jersey* (New York: Lewis Historical Publishing, 1910), vol. 3: 1280–81. For Hagar's manumission, see Burlington County, *Manumissions of Slaves,* Book B (1820–1853), p. 35, New Jersey Department of State Archives. Hagar was thirty-three at the time of her freedom.

7. Arthur Zilversmit, *The First Emancipation* (Chicago: University of Chicago Press, 1967); Graham Russell Hodges, *Slavery and Freedom in the Rural North: African Americans in Monmouth County, New Jersey, 1665–1865* (Madison, WI: Madison House, 1997). For evidence of kidnapping in Burlington County, see M. M. Pernot, ed., *After Freedom* (Burlington, NJ: Burlington County Historical Society, 1987).

8. For Gideon Morehouse in Cayuga County, see Town of Genoa, Cayuga County, Bureau of Census, Third Census (1810). For his church membership, see "Records of First Presbyterian Church of Ludlowville, New York, 1817–1832," in possession of Louise Bement, Cornell University. On the area's division, see Jane Marsh Dieckmann, *A Short History of Tompkins County* (Ithaca, NY: DeWitt Historical Society of Tompkins County, 1986), 76–78, and Carol Kammen, *The Peopling of Tompkins County: A Social History* (Interlaken, NY: Heart of the Lakes, 1985), 70–73. For Morehouse's properties, see "Books of Deeds," Tompkins County Clerk's Office, Ithaca, Books C: 407; X: 293–95; DD: 253, and "Last Will of Gideon Morehouse and Genealogical Data on the Morehouse Family," in possession of Louise Bement. See also the articles on Morehouse and Wheeler in "Newsletter of Lansing Historical Association" (Lansing, NY: Lansing Historical Society, 1998).

9. For slavery in Ludlowville, see Alice Adele Bristol, "The History of Ludlowville, A Village of the Finger Lakes Region Located in Lansing Township of Tompkins County, New York," typescript, DeWitt Historical Society of Tompkins County, 82–83. Included in this history is a brief account of Big Tom, another slave owned by Morehouse. For local slavery, see Sidney Gallwey, *Peter Webb: Slave-Freeman-Citizen of Tompkins County, New York* (Ithaca, NY: DeWitt Historical Society of Tompkins County, 1960), and Gallwey, *Early Slaves and Freemen of Tompkins County* (Ithaca, NY: Ithaca Council for Equality, 1962).

10. See Phyllis F. Field, *The Politics of Race in New York: The Struggle for Black Suffrage in the Civil War Era* (Ithaca, NY: Cornell University Press, 1982).

11. Wheeler gives the date of the eclipse as June 6, 1810; the event actually took place on June 16, 1810. See *Utica Patriot,* June 10, 1810.

12. For accusation, see District Attorney Indictment Papers, Reel 16 (August 16–December 4, 1806), New York Municipal Archives and Records Center.

13. Jeffrey Bolster, *Black Jacks: African American Seamen in the Age of Sail* (Cambridge: Harvard University Press, 1997), 235. On domestics, see Shane White, *Somewhat More Independent: The End of Slavery in New York City, 1770–1810* (Athens:

University of Georgia Press, 1991), and Elizabeth Blackmar, *Manhattan for Rent, 1785–1850* (Ithaca, NY: Cornell University Press, 1989), 57–59, 112–15.

14. Fifth Census (1830) Population of New York 4 (Columbia County), p. 179. For a detailed study of these patterns, see Martin Bruegel, *Farm, Shop, Landing: The Rise of a Market Society in the Hudson Valley, 1780–1860* (Durham, NC: Duke University Press, 2002), 144–45. Michael Edward Groth, "Forging Freedom in the Mid-Hudson Valley: The End of Slavery and the Formation of a Free African-American Community in Dutchess County, New York, 1770–1850," PhD diss. Binghamton University, 1994, and John Brooke, *Columbia: Civil Life on the Upper Hudson from the Revolution to the Age of Jackson* (Chapel Hill: University of North Carolina Press for the Omohundro Institute of Early American History and Culture, 2009). I am grateful to Professor Brooke for allowing me to look at his splendid manuscript on Columbia County. For Spencertown, see Charles S. Davenport, "Interesting Facts Connected with Spencertown's Early History," typescript, 1923, Chatham Public Library, and Austerlitz Town Files, Columbia County Historical Society, Kinderhook.

15. For a discussion of Williams's narrative, see Blassingame, "Using the Testimony of Ex-Slaves," 81.

16. Davenport, "Interesting Facts," 5–6.

17. Ibid., 66–67.

18. Evidence as to the date of Wheeler's death is contradictory; this date is from Milton Halsey Thomas, *The Records of St. Peter's Presbyterian Church of Spencertown, Columbia County, New York* (New York: n.p., 1925), 9. Yet another source lists Wheeler and his wife, Sylvia, as admitted to the church in 1843; see St. Peter's Presbyterian Church, Spencertown, New York, Records 12, 18, Columbia County Historical Society, Kinderhook. For Morehouse's death, see *New York Genealogical and Biographical Record* (192), 369. Morehouse died at the age of seventy-one.

19. Charles Lester, *Mountain Wild Forever; Or, Memoirs of Mrs. Mary Ann Bise, a Lady Who Died at the Age of Twenty-three in the Valley of the Green River* (New York: E. French, 1838); *Columbia County at the End of the Century*, vol. 2: 706–08.

20. For activities at the World Anti-Slavery Convention, see "Minute Book for the General Convention [British] Anti-Slavery Papers," vol. C/1/18 (1840), 48, 50, 97, Mss. British Empire 5/16/24, Rhodes Library, Oxford University. See also Charles Lester, *History of Twelve Thousand Fugitive Slaves Who Have Emancipated Themselves by Flight* (London: Manning and Mason, 1840). For Hiram Wilson, see Jane H. Pease and William H. Pease, *Bound with Them in Chains: A Biographical History of the Antislavery Movement* (Westport, CT: Greenwood Press, 1972), 115–40.

21. For a discussion of the debate between Lester and Brown, see Allen P. Stouffer, *The Light and Nature and the Law of God: Antislavery in Ontario, 1833–1877* (Baton Rouge: Louisiana State University Press, 1992), 73–75.

22. For the review of *The Glory and Shame of England*, see *Colored American* (*Weekly Advocate*) (New York), December 25, 1841.

23. James Grant Wilson and John Fiske, eds., *Appleton's Cyclopedia of American Biography* (New York: D. Appleton and Company, 1888). John Blassingame is the sole critic of slave narratives to recognize Lester's career as a historian. See Blassingame, "Using the Testimony of Ex-Slaves," 80.

24. For methods of amanuensis, see Blassingame, "Using the Testimony of Ex-Slaves," 80–81, and Andrews, *To Tell a Free Story,* 83–85.

25. See *National Era* (Washington, DC), August 8, 1850. For Lester and Brady, see Mary Panzer, *Matthew Brady and the Image of History* (Washington, DC: Smithsonian Institution Press, 1997), 10, 33, 43, 55, 52, 64–65, 76, 173.

26. *Frederick Douglass' Paper* (Rochester, NY), February 19, 1852.

27. Hosea Easton, *A Treatise on the Intellectual Character and Civil and Political Condition of the Colored People of the U. States and the Prejudice Exercised Towards Them* (Boston: Isaac Knapp, 1837), 41.

28. See Sterling Stuckey, *Slave Culture: Nationalist Theory and the Foundations of Black America* (New York: Oxford University Press, 1987), 198.

29. On Northrup, see Robert Burns Stepto, "I Rose and Found My Voice: Narration, Authentication, and Authorial Control in Four Slave Narratives," in Davis and Gates Jr., *Slave's Narrative,* 225–41. On self-effacing, see Andrews, *To Tell a Free Story,* 86. Wheeler is referring to [Charles Ball], *Slavery in the United States: a narrative of the life and adventures of Charles Ball, a black man, who lived forty years in Maryland, South Carolina and Georgia, as a slave, under various masters, and was one year in the navy with Commodore Barney, during the late war. Containing an account of the manners and usages of the planters and slaveholders of the South—a description of the condition and treatment of the slaves, with observations upon the state of morals amongst the cotton planters, and the perils and sufferings of a fugitive slave, who twice escaped from the cotton country* (New York: Published by John S. Taylor, 1837). For a similar narrative, see [William Grimes], *Life of William Grimes, the Runaway Slave. Written by Himself* (New York: [W. Grimes], 1825).

30. See discussion of Mr. Covey's importance to Douglass in Donald B. Gibson, "Faith, Doubt, and Apostasy: Evidence of Things Unseen in Frederick Douglass's Narrative," in Eric J. Sundquist, ed., *Frederick Douglass: New Literary and Historical Essays* (New York: Cambridge University Press, 1990), 84–99.

31. On the road to salvation in narratives, see Angelo Costanzo, *Surprizing Narrative: Olaudah Equiano and the Beginnings of Black Autobiography* (Westport, CT: Greenwood Press, 1987), and for Bunyan, see Thomas R. Cole, *The Journey of Life: A Cultural History of Aging in America* (New York: Cambridge University Press, 1992).

32. See Wilson Jeremiah Moses, *Alexander Crummell: A Study of Civilization and Discontent* (New York: Oxford University Press, 1989), and David E. Swift, *Black Prophets of Justice: Activist Clergy before the Civil War* (Baton Rouge: Louisiana State University Press, 1989).

33. On the ring shout, see Stuckey, *Slave Culture,* 12, 24, 36, 89, 96, and Hodges, *Black Itinerants of the Gospel,* 36–39.

34. Bristol, "History of Ludlowville," 27, 30, 134–38, 185–87.

35. For double veil, see W. E. B. Du Bois, *The Souls of Black Folks* (New York: McClurg and Co., 1903). For African sources of spirituality, see Wyatt McGaffey, *Religion and Society in Central Africa: The Bakongo of Lower Zaire* (Chicago: University of Chicago Press, 1986).